Present Yourself 1

Experiences

Steven Gershon

CAMBRIDGE
UNIVERSITY PRESS

CAMBRIDGE UNIVERSITY PRESS
Cambridge, New York, Melbourne, Madrid, Cape Town, Singapore, São Paulo, Delhi

Cambridge University Press
32 Avenue of the Americas, New York, NY 10013-2473, USA

www.cambridge.org
Information on this title: www.cambridge.org/9780521713283

First published 2008

Printed in Hong Kong, China, by Golden Cup Printing Company Limited

A catalog record for this publication is available from the British Library

Library of Congress Cataloging-in-Publication Data
Gershon, Steven.
 Present yourself 1: experiences / Steven Gershon.
    p. cm.
 Summary: "Present Yourself is a presentation skills course for adult and young adult learners of English,
 developed within the framework of a general conversation course" – Provided by publisher.
 ISBN 978-0-521-71328-3
 1. English language – Textbooks for foreign speakers. I. Title. II. Title: Present yourself one.

PE1128.G39 2008
428.0076 – dc22

2008027117

ISBN 978-0-521-71328-3 student's book and audio CD
ISBN 978-0-521-71329-0 teacher's manual

Art direction, book design, photo research, and layout services: Adventure House, NYC
Audio production: Richard LePage and Associates

Contents

Plan of the book

Getting ready pages 2–7	**Preparing to present** Doing a survey to get to know classmates Learning about the steps for a presentation	**Giving a self-introduction** Completing a brainstorming map Learning about the organization of a presentation Listening to a self-introduction

Unit	**Topic** focus	**Language** focus	**Organization** focus
1 **A new club member** pages 8–19	Talking about people's personal profiles Completing a personal profile questionnaire about yourself and a classmate	Words to describe people Talking about interests	All units include focusing on brainstorming ideas and creating an outline for a presentation.
2 **A favorite place** pages 20–31	Words to describe places Interviewing classmates about favorite places	Describing places Talking about activities	
3 **A prized possession** pages 32–43	Discussing what makes some possessions important Doing a survey about classmates' possessions	Words to describe possessions Describing possessions Explaining the history of a possession	
4 **A memorable experience** pages 44–55	Words to describe experiences and feelings Interviewing classmates about memorable experiences	Setting the scene Using time expressions to tell a story	
5 **Show me how.** pages 56–67	Discussing skills and talents Doing a survey about classmates' skills and talents	Presenting the materials you need Giving instructions	
6 **Movie magic** pages 68–79	Taking a movie quiz Discussing movie highlights	Talking about movies Words to describe movie features	

Presentation tips	**My self-introduction**
An introduction to what good presenters do	Preparing and giving a self-introduction

Presentation focus	**Presentation skills** focus	**Present yourself!**
All units include focusing on the introduction, body, and conclusion of a presentation, and listening to a model presentation.	Stage presence techniques Tip: Speaking from notes	Interviewing a classmate Creating an outline Giving a classmate introduction
	Gestures for describing size and shape Tip: Exaggerating gestures	Brainstorming ideas Creating an outline Giving a presentation about a favorite place
	Show-and-tell expressions Tip: Steps for presenting an object to an audience	Brainstorming ideas Creating an outline Giving a presentation about a prized possession
	Using stress and emphasis with *really*, *so*, and *very* Tip: Saying intensifiers slowly	Brainstorming ideas Creating an outline Giving a presentation about a memorable experience
	Emphasizing key points Tip: Steps for giving instructions effectively	Brainstorming ideas Creating an outline Demonstrating a skill or talent
	Using stress and emphasis with *absolutely*, *extremely*, *incredibly*, and *surprisingly* Tip: Saying intensifiers loudly	Brainstorming ideas Creating an outline Reviewing a movie

To the teacher

In our rapidly globalizing world, effective communication skills are becoming more and more important for success – academically, professionally, socially, and personally. The way we interact within a group can affect the quality and success of our relationships. Just as important, the effectiveness with which we communicate in front of a group can have a great impact on our achievements in the world – opening many doors of opportunity and rewarding possibility. The *Present Yourself* series focuses on developing students' communication skills so that they have the confidence to take advantage of the many opportunities in their lives to present their ideas, experiences, knowledge, and opinions in front of a group.

Present Yourself offers a process approach that emphasizes the interdependent step-by-step decisions and tasks that are involved in planning, writing, and delivering an effective presentation to an audience. These steps include selecting a suitable topic; considering the language needed to talk about the topic; brainstorming ideas for the content of the presentation; organizing the ideas into an introduction, body, and conclusion; employing specific physical and verbal skills to enhance the delivery of the presentation; and, finally, completing a self-evaluation once the presentation has been given. Throughout this step-by-step process, the main goal is to provide students with a readily transferable set of skills they can use to give effective presentations on a range of topics in a variety of situations.

Present Yourself 1, Experiences focuses on topics that encourage students to speak from personal experience. The book includes six main units and one introductory unit. The introductory unit acquaints students with the process of planning a presentation and offers an entry point to giving a presentation by having students give a self-introduction. Each of the six main units guides students through the entire presentation process with engaging speaking activities, focused listening tasks that provide relevant topic input, and clear functional language support that targets both vocabulary and useful sentence patterns. Moreover, the core of each unit provides a complete model presentation that students use to help them construct their own presentations based on that unit's topic.

The topics of the six main units are loosely graded in level of difficulty, ranging from a classmate introduction in unit one, to a demonstration in unit four, to a movie review in unit six. However, as we all know, every class is different, so please feel free to pick and choose units according to your students' interests, class level, and available time.

I hope you and your students enjoy *Present Yourself*. I have enjoyed writing it and wish you success with presentations in your classroom.

Regards,

Steve Gershon

How a unit works

Each unit contains six lessons to guide students through the process of building an effective and engaging presentation. Each lesson, with the exception of the first lesson, builds on the previous one in order to provide students with the necessary skills to create and deliver their own presentations.

Topic focus

This lesson helps students to think about the topic and what they already know about it. The activities introduce useful topic-based vocabulary and encourage students to interact with each other through surveys, questionnaires, quizzes, and interviews. When students finish this lesson, they will have generated ideas that they can use later in the unit when they begin to plan their own presentations.

Language focus

This lesson encourages students to notice useful target expressions and sentence patterns they can use to talk about the unit topic. Students also listen to different speakers use the target language in the context of giving a presentation, and perform task-based listening activities. Students consolidate the target language through a semicontrolled speaking activity at the end of the lesson.

Organization focus

This lesson teaches students how to select ideas from a brainstorming map and organize them into a presentation outline that includes an introduction, a body, and a conclusion. Students are asked to notice which ideas from a brainstorming map have been included as main topics in an outline and to complete the outline with additional notes. Finally, students have an opportunity to listen to the complete presentation as they check the completed outline.

Presentation focus

In this lesson students focus on a model presentation written from the outline in the **Organization focus**. Students focus on the introduction, body, and conclusion of the presentation to see what information is included in each section. While looking at a cloze version of the model presentation, students predict the items to complete each section. They then listen to the complete presentation and check their answers.

Presentation skills focus

At this stage of the unit, students are ready to focus on a specific linguistic or physical skill related to the actual delivery of their presentation. In each unit the presentation skill is first presented visually. The order of the following activities varies depending on the presentation skill, but in every unit students read a section of a presentation to observe the presentation skill in action. They also have an opportunity to practice the presentation skill with a partner, or in a group, in a controlled speaking activity.

Present yourself!

In the last lesson of the unit, students plan, organize, and give their own presentations based on the unit topic. First, students brainstorm ideas for their topic and create an outline for their presentation. Then they practice on their own before giving their presentations to the whole class or in a group. A self-evaluation form for each unit is included at the back of the book for students to evaluate their own presentations once they're finished.

Author's acknowledgments

I would like to thank the following reviewers for their valuable insights and suggestions:

Yasmine Bia, **ELS Language Centers**, Vancouver, British Columbia, Canada; Madonna Carr, **University of Illinois at Chicago**, Chicago, Illinois, U.S.A.; Frank Claypool, **Osaka College of Foreign Languages**, Osaka, Japan; Karen Cronin; Alison Doughtie, **Mohawk Valley Community College**, Utica, New York, U.S.A.; Kirvin Andrew Dyer, **Yan-Ping High School**, Taipei, Taiwan; Karen Englander, **Universidad Autónoma de Baja California**, Baja California, Mexico; Lisa Feasby, **Korea University**, Seoul, South Korea; Denise Fenwick, **Kobe Women's University**, Kobe, Japan; Duane Gerussi, **Kansai Gaidai University**, Osaka, Japan; Linda Gogliotti, **Aichi University**, Aichi, Japan; Oscar Gutiérrez Pulido; Angela Harris, **Tennessee Foreign Language Institute**, Nashville, Tennessee, U.S.A.; Ray Hartman, **Sungkyunkwan University**, Seoul, South Korea; Midori Iba, **Konan University**, Kobe, Japan; Kanae Koike; Yayoi Kosugi, **Keio University**, **Tokyo Eiwa Women's University**, Tokyo, Japan; Masashi Kubono; Susan Lafond, **Guilderland High School**, Guilderland, New York, U.S.A.; Huei-Chih Christine Liu, **Shu-Te University**, Kaohsiung County, Taiwan; David McMurray, **The International University of Kagoshima**, Kagoshima, Japan; Kazuhiro Nomura, **Kobe City University of Foreign Studies**, Kobe, Japan; Geraldine Norris, **University of Shizuoka**, Shizuoka, Japan; Mark Senior, **Konan University**, Kobe, Japan; and Rena Yoshida, **J.F. Oberlin University**, Tokyo, Japan.

A special thanks to the **editorial** and **production** team at Cambridge University Press who worked on this course:

Sue Aldcorn, Karen Brock, Sarah Cole, Brigit Dermott, Deborah Goldblatt, Vivian Gomez, Louisa Hellegers, Alejandro Martinez, Julia Meuse, Kathy Niemczyk, Sandra Pike, Christie Polchowski, Kate Powers, Tami Savir, Jaimie Scanlon, Satoko Shimoyama, Rachel Sinden, Lori Solbakken, and Shelagh Speers.

Thanks to the Cambridge University Press **staff** and **advisors**:

Harry Ahn, Yumiko Akeba, Kenneth Clinton, Heather Gray, Tomomi Katsuki, Jennifer Kim, Robert Kim, Kareen Kjelstrup, John Letcher, Hugo Loyola, Andy Martin, Carine Mitchell, Catherine Shih, Howard Siegelman, Ivan Sorrentino, Herman Su, Irene Yang, and Ellen Zlotnick.

I would like to express my sincere thanks to Richard Walker for his participation in this project as a contributing writer. As well, I would like to thank all of my "Techniques in Speech" students at J.F. Oberlin University, from whom I continue to learn how to teach presentation skills. Finally, my thanks to Britt and Becky, who never fail to offer useful suggestions whenever I ask them to "have a look at this activity and tell me what you think."

To the student

Dear students:

What is your greatest fear? Seeing a big spider? Walking alone on a dark street? Having a serious illness? Being in an earthquake? These are some of the answers that people often give in popular magazine surveys. Surprisingly, the one fear that seems to be on everyone's top-ten list is public speaking. That's right. Most people say that giving a presentation to a group of people is more frightening than seeing a spider, having an illness, or being in an earthquake!

People's fear of public speaking is understandable for a few reasons. First, when we give a presentation, we feel that we are being judged. And nobody wants to sound foolish or be boring – especially in front of a lot of people. Moreover, giving a good presentation involves a variety of communication skills that are very complex – even for native speakers. And of course it is even more difficult (and frightening!) when you are speaking a foreign language, with so much new vocabulary and grammar to remember.

For learners of English, giving a good presentation involves more than using English correctly. It involves choosing a suitable topic for your audience and deciding what you want to say. It also involves organizing your ideas into an attention-getting introduction (beginning), a clear body (middle), and a memorable conclusion (end). And, finally, it involves using your voice, gestures, posture, and eye contact to connect with the audience. All of these skills seem like a lot to learn, but with study and practice anyone can master the skills to be a great presenter!

So, why is it useful to learn presentation skills? It's simply because most of us will have to give a presentation or speech at some time in our life – whether we want to or not. It may be for school, work, a conference, or for a social occasion, such as a wedding, party, or club event. The purpose may be to share something personal about someone or yourself, to inform an audience about a specific topic, to explain how to make or do something, or to persuade people to change their opinion on a topic. Whatever the purpose, any time we speak to a group of people about a topic, we are giving a presentation. This means that presentation skills are very useful life skills.

Present Yourself 1, Experiences will introduce you to the communication skills you need to speak clearly, effectively, and confidently in front of any group – small or large. I hope you have fun using *Present Yourself*, and I am sure your classmates will enjoy the presentations you give.

Good luck!

Steve Gershon

Getting ready

Preparing to present

1 My classmates, my audience

A Complete the survey below. Ask a different classmate each question. Write the classmate's name below.

"Are you from a small town?"

"Do you . . . ?"   *"Have you . . . ?"*   *"Can you . . . ?"*

Find someone who . . .	Classmate
is from a small town	James
is good at sports	
has been abroad	
can play an instrument	
has a pet	
belongs to a club	
is a little nervous about taking this class	

B Tell the class about some of your classmates.

"James is from a small town. Min Hee enjoys . . . "

2 Presentation steps

A Look at these students in a presentation class. What are they doing to prepare for their presentations?

B 2   Read the presentation steps. Put them in order from 1 to 6. Then listen and check your answers.

_____ Choose the main topics to include. Then brainstorm and write details about each topic.

_1_ Think about the audience's needs and interests.

_____ Organize the main topics and details into an outline with an introduction, a body, and a conclusion.

_____ Practice your presentation many times.

_____ Brainstorm and write lots of topics and information.

_____ Make final notes to use for your presentation.

Giving a self-introduction

1 Brainstorming

A Read Carmen's brainstorming notes for her self-introduction presentation. Then check (✓) the four topics she included in her brainstorming map below.

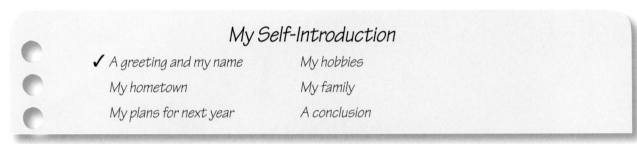

My Self-Introduction

✓ A greeting and my name   My hobbies

  My hometown   My family

  My plans for next year   A conclusion

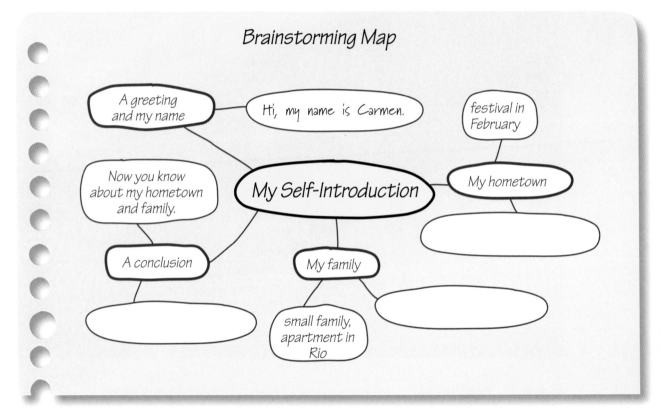

Brainstorming Map

A greeting and my name — Hi, my name is Carmen.

festival in February

Now you know about my hometown and family.

My Self-Introduction

My hometown

A conclusion

My family

small family, apartment in Rio

B Read Carmen's additional notes for her presentation. Then use her notes to complete the brainstorming map in Exercise A.

- Thank you for listening.
- beautiful city, beaches, mountains
- brother, high school student
- ✓ Hi, my name is Carmen.

Organizing

A Notice the information Carmen included in her presentation.

▶ A greeting and her name

▶ The topics she wants to talk about and a few details about each one
Today I'm going to tell you about . . .

   ▶ Her hometown
   I'm from . . .   It has . . .   We have . . .

   ▶ Her family
   I have a small / big family.   We live . . .   I have one brother / sister.

▶ A conclusion
Now you know a little about my . . .   Thank you for listening.

B 🔘 3   Guess the missing words in Carmen's presentation. Then listen and check your guesses.

My Self-Introduction

Hi, my _____name_____ is Carmen. Today I'm

going to tell you about my hometown and my family.

I'm _____ Rio de Janeiro, in Brazil. Rio

is a beautiful city. It has great beaches and it's

surrounded by mountains. In February, we have a

wonderful festival called Carnaval. I have a small family.

We _____ in an apartment in Rio.

I have one brother. His name is Marco and he's a high

school student. Now you _____ a little

about my hometown and family. _____

_____ for listening.

Presentation tips

A Work with a partner. Match the tips to the pictures.

✓ a. Speak loudly and clearly.   d. Maintain good posture.
   b. Use gestures to show meaning.   e. Make eye contact.
   c. Stress important words.   f. Relax and smile.

3. a

B Choose two tips you think are important. Tell a partner.

*"I think two important tips are 'Make eye contact' and 'Speak loudly and clearly.'
How about you?"*

My self-introduction

Prepare and give a one-minute presentation.

A Complete the brainstorming map with topics and information you want to include in your presentation.

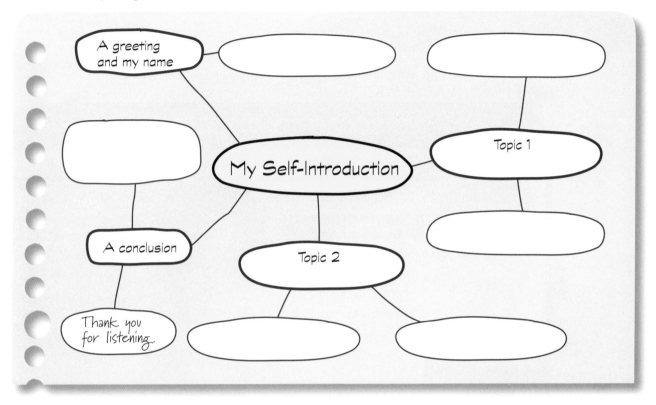

B Use your brainstorming map to complete these notes for your presentation.

	My Self-Introduction
A greeting and my name	
Topic 1 and a few details	
Topic 2 and a few details	
A conclusion	

C Make final notes for your presentation on a separate piece of paper. When you finish, practice your presentation silently a few times. Then practice out loud with a partner.

D Work in groups. Take turns giving your presentations.

1 A new club member

1 People

A Read the personal profiles. Which person would you most like to meet? Why?
Tell a partner.

"I'd like to meet Seiji. He's my age."

Welcome to *myclub.cup!*

Check out these personal profiles.

Hi, I'm Seiji.

About me

Age 22

Occupation sales
representative

Hometown Tokyo

Interests writing a
blog, surfing the Net

Hi, I'm Melissa.

About me

Age 25

Occupation teacher

Hometown Sydney

Interests taking
photos, going to
museums

Hi, I'm Matt.

About me

Age 20

Occupation student

Hometown
Los Angeles

Interests playing
soccer and baseball

Hi, I'm Sophia.

About me

Age 19

Occupation student

Hometown Paris

Interests listening
to hip-hop music,
dancing

B Do you have anything in common with these people? Tell your partner.

"I have something in common with Seiji. I'm from Tokyo, too."
  "I don't have anything in common with these people. I'm 23. I'm from . . . "

2 All about you

A Complete the questionnaire about yourself. Then ask a partner the questions. Write your partner's answers.

Personal Profile Questionnaire

Tell us about . . .

you	Me	My partner
What's your name?	Peter	Lucy
Where are you from?		
What do you do?		
Do you have a part-time job? If *yes*, write the job.		
your family		
How many brothers or sisters do you have?		
Are they older or younger?		
your interests		
What do you like doing in your free time?		
your favorites		
What's your favorite food? music? movie? place to hang out?		

B Join another pair of students. Tell them three interesting things about your partner.

"My partner is Lucy. She has two older brothers. Her favorite food is . . . "

Language focus

1 Personalities

A 💿 4 How do these people describe themselves? Complete the sentences with words from the box. Then listen and check your guesses.

Words to describe people			
active	outgoing	smart	_____
creative	✓ shy	talkative	_____

1. I like spending time alone. I'm very ___shy___ .

2. I love meeting new people. I'm really _____ .

3. I enjoy playing sports and being outdoors. I'm very _____ .

B What other words describe people? Add more words to the box in Exercise A. Then compare words with a partner.

2 My self-description

A Complete the chart with words that describe you. Give examples for each word.

Word	Examples
active	like playing sports, enjoy hiking, camping
_____	_____
_____	_____

B Work with a partner. Take turns describing yourselves.

"I'm very active. I like playing sports, and I enjoy . . . "

3 Different interests

A Read the list of people's interests. Then add your own ideas.

Interests

chatting online	playing tennis	_____
going shopping	playing the piano	_____
going to the movies	singing karaoke	_____

B 🔘 5 Now listen to some friends talk about Nick, Jin Su, and Ali. What are their interests? Check (✓) two interests for each person.

1. Nick   ☑ playing the piano   ☐ writing a blog   ☑ watching sports

2. Jin Su   ☐ hanging out with friends   ☐ eating out   ☐ going shopping

3. Ali   ☐ swimming   ☐ skydiving   ☐ going to the movies

4 Class interests

A Complete the chart. Ask three classmates about their interests.

"What do you like doing in your free time?"
    "I like surfing and playing the guitar."

Classmate	Interests
Ken	surfing, playing the guitar
1	
2	
3	

B Tell the class about your classmates' interests.

"Ken loves surfing. He also likes . . . "

Talking about interests

He likes	playing the guitar.
He loves	surfing.
She enjoys	eating out.
She's into	skydiving.

Organization focus

1   Alison introduces her classmate Kate

A Look at the picture of Kate's kitchen. What do you think she likes doing in her free time?

B First, Alison brainstormed interview topics and questions for her presentation about Kate. Read the topics. Then write questions for the topics.

Topics for interview with Kate   Questions

Occupation   _____

Hometown   _____

Family   _____

Personality   *How would you describe yourself?*

Interests   _____

Favorite food   _____

Future goals   *What are your future goals?*

C Alison interviewed Kate and took notes. Read the notes. Where do they go in Alison's outline on page 13? Complete the outline.

- now lives in Taipei
- hanging out with friends, going shopping, chatting
- has a younger brother, two older sisters
- makes chocolate fudge

- really active, always busy
- to meet Maria Sharapova, play tennis
- third-year student, studying tourism

2 Alison's outline

⊙ 6 Listen to Alison's presentation. Check the notes you added from Exercise 1C on page 12.

Introducing Kate

I. Introduction

    A. Introduce Kate: I'm pleased to introduce my friend Kate.

    B. Kate's occupation: _____

    C. Her hometown

        1. originally from Jiou Fen, small town outside of Taipei

        2. _____

    D. Her family

        1. _____

        2. parents live in Jiou Fen, own traditional teahouse

II. Body

    A. Kate's personality

        1. very friendly and outgoing, loves meeting new people

        2. _____

    B. Her interests

        1. _____

        2. into playing sports, loves swimming, playing tennis after school

    C. Her favorite food: chocolate

        1. eats chocolate candy, cookies, ice cream

        2. _____

III. Conclusion

    Kate's future goals

        1. to travel, learn about other cultures

        2. to work for an international hotel chain

        3. _____

Presentation focus

1 Introduction

A Notice the information Alison included in the introduction of her presentation on page 15.

> ▶ A sentence introducing the person
> *I'm pleased to introduce my friend . . .*
>
> ▶ The person's
>   • occupation
>   • hometown
>   • family

B 💿 7 Guess the missing words in Alison's introduction. Then listen and check your guesses.

2 Body

A Notice the information Alison included in the body of her presentation on page 15.

> ▶ A description of the person's personality
>
> ▶ The person's interests
>
> ▶ One of the person's favorite things

B 💿 8 Guess the missing words in the body of Alison's presentation. Then listen and check your guesses.

3 Conclusion

A Notice the information Alison included in the conclusion of her presentation on page 15.

> ▶ The person's future goals
> *Someday, she wants to . . .*   *Her dream is to . . .*

B 💿 9 Guess the missing words in Alison's conclusion. Then listen and check your guesses.

Introducing Kate

Introduction

Hi. I'm pleased to introduce my friend Kate to you today. Kate's a third-year university student, and she's studying tourism. She's originally from Jiou Fen, a small town outside of Taipei, but now she _____ in Taipei. She _____ a younger brother and two older sisters. Kate's parents _____ in Jiou Fen, and they own a traditional teahouse there.

Body

So, how would I describe Kate? Well, she's very friendly and outgoing. She loves meeting new people. Kate's also really active. She's always busy. In her free time she enjoys _____ _____ with friends. She likes going shopping with them on weekends, or chatting in a coffee shop or restaurant. She's _____ playing sports, and she loves swimming or _____ tennis after school. Here's something interesting about Kate: her _____ food is chocolate. She eats chocolate candy, chocolate cookies, chocolate ice cream, and she even makes chocolate fudge! She loves eating all kinds of chocolate.

Conclusion

What about Kate's future goals? Well, she's studying tourism because she wants to travel and _____ about other cultures. Someday, she wants to work for an international organization, maybe an international _____ chain. Her dream is to meet Maria Sharapova and play a game of tennis with her! Let's welcome Kate to our class! Thank you.

Presentation skills focus

1 Stage presence techniques

Stage presence means creating a positive connection with audience members and keeping their attention. Use these techniques to help you develop your stage presence.

Look at the pictures and read the information. Then practice with a partner. Stand up and try each technique.

Relax before you begin.
• Take slow, deep breaths.
• Smile at your audience.

Speak loudly and clearly.
• Make sure the audience can hear you.
• Speak slowly. Don't rush.

Make eye contact.
• Try to look at the entire audience.
• Then make eye contact with specific audience members.

Maintain good posture.
• Place your feet about 30 centimeters (12 inches) apart.
• Don't move from side to side.

Presentation tip

Don't read directly from your notes. When you need to check your notes, pause briefly, look at your notes, and then look up at the audience and continue speaking.

2 Your turn

A Read the example from a presentation about a new club member.

> So, how would I describe Sara? She's very creative. She enjoys painting and drawing pictures. She's a little shy sometimes, especially when she meets new people. Sara loves studying, and she's a really good student, so I think she's really smart. Her favorite place to hang out is Bean Café. She goes there after school almost every day.

B Work with a partner. Take turns reading the example in Exercise A aloud. Practice stage presence techniques and speaking from notes.

C Think of a person you know well. Complete the information.

I'm going to tell you about my _____ .

Name: His / Her name is _____ .

Occupation: He's / She's a(n) _____ .

Hometown: He's / She's from _____ .

Interests: He / She enjoys _____ and _____ .

A favorite: His / Her favorite _____ is _____ .

D Work in groups. Take turns introducing the person from Exercise C. Use the stage presence techniques on page 16.

"I'm going to tell you about my brother. His name is Tom . . . "

Now **present yourself!**

- **Turn to page 18.**
- **Prepare your presentation.**

Present yourself!

Introduce a classmate to the class.

[1] Brainstorming

A Find a classmate to interview. Write the classmate's name in the center of the brainstorming map. Then brainstorm questions for each interview topic.

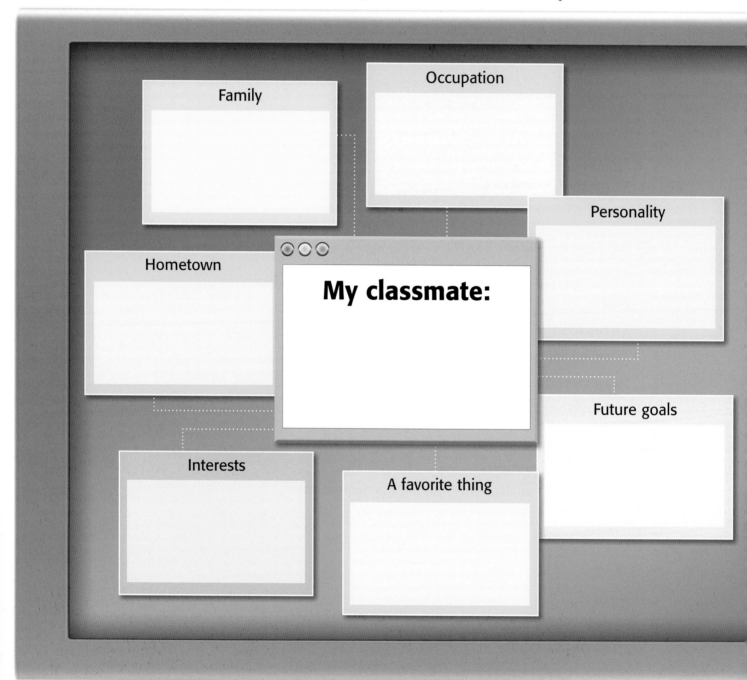

Family

Occupation

Personality

Hometown

My classmate:

Future goals

Interests

A favorite thing

B Use your topics and questions from Exercise A to interview your partner. Take notes on a separate piece of paper.

2 Organizing

Use your interview notes from Exercise 1B to complete the outline. Then make note cards from your outline and practice your presentation.

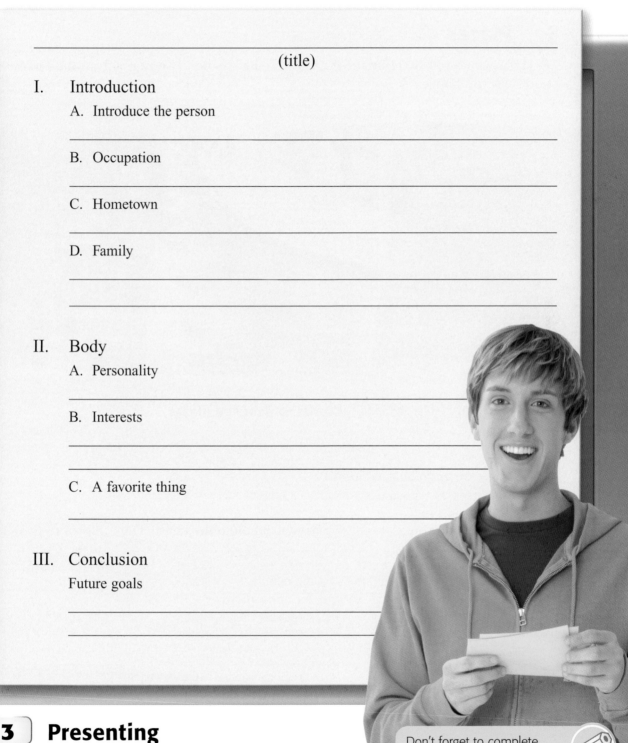

_____
(title)

I. Introduction
   A. Introduce the person
   _____

   B. Occupation
   _____

   C. Hometown
   _____

   D. Family
   _____
   _____

II. Body
   A. Personality
   _____

   B. Interests
   _____
   _____

   C. A favorite thing
   _____

III. Conclusion
   Future goals
   _____
   _____

3 Presenting

Give your presentation to the class.
Remember to use stage presence techniques.

Don't forget to complete your self-evaluation on page 80 after your presentation.

2 A favorite place

1 Places

A How would you describe these places? Tell a partner. Use words from the box and ones you know.

Words to describe places

beautiful	crowded	messy	noisy	peaceful	spacious
clean	lively	neat and tidy	old-fashioned	small and cozy	trendy

"I think the park looks beautiful."

B How often do you go to these places? Complete the chart. Then tell your partner.

an amusement park	a café	a movie theater	a park
a beach	a club	a museum	a shopping mall

at least once a week	once a month or more	once or twice a year
_____	_____	_____
_____	_____	_____
_____	_____	_____

"I go to an amusement park once or twice a year. How about you?"

C Where else do you spend time? Tell your partner.

2 Favorite places

A Complete the chart with information about your favorite places.

Where do you go to . . . ?	Place	Description	How often I go there
get a good cup of coffee	Joe's Coffee Shop	busy, trendy	at least once a week
take a long walk			
get out of the house on a rainy day			
get an afternoon snack			
hang out with friends			
listen to live music			
window shop			

B Work with a partner. Take turns asking each other about the places in Exercise A. Take notes on a separate piece of paper.

A Where do you go to *get a good cup of coffee*?

B *Joe's Coffee Shop*. I love that place.

A Really? What's it like?

B It's *busy*, and it's very *trendy*.

A So, how often do you go there?

B *At least once a week.*

C Join another pair of students. Tell them about some of your partner's favorite places.

"To get a good cup of coffee, Jin goes to . . . "

Language focus

1 What's it like?

A 💿 10 Listen to Carlos, Alice, and Emma describe their favorite places. Number the pictures from 1 to 3. (There is one extra picture.)

B 💿 10 Listen again. Check (✔) the words you hear.

1. Carlos   ☐ peaceful   ☐ trees   ☐ flowers   ☐ a bench

2. Alice   ☐ small and cozy   ☐ noisy   ☐ a table   ☐ pictures

3. Emma   ☐ spacious   ☐ messy   ☐ a chair   ☐ a rug

C What's your home like? Write two true sentences and two false sentences on a separate piece of paper. Use the language for describing places.

> It's spacious.
> It has a new kitchen.
> There's . . .

Describing places	
It's	spacious. small and cozy.
It has	a new kitchen. great views.
There's	a computer. an armchair.
There are	lots of windows. tall trees.

D Work in groups. Take turns reading your sentences. Your classmates say *True* or *False*. For false sentences, give the correct information.

A It's *spacious*.

B True.

A That's false. It's *small and cozy*.

2 It's a great place to . . .

A Read the list of activities people do at their favorite places. Then add one more idea.

Activities

____ do homework   ____ get some fresh air   ____ surf the Net

_C_ enjoy a good book   ____ hang out with friends   ____ watch people

____ get away from it all   _C_ relax   _____

B 🔘 11 Listen. What two activities do Carlos, Alice, and Emma do?
Write *C* (Carlos), *A* (Alice), or *E* (Emma) next to their activities in Exercise A.

3 My favorite places

A Complete the chart with information about two of your favorite places.

Place	Description	Activities
City Center Mall	lots of shops, a video arcade	hang out with friends, shop for clothes
①		
②		

B Work with a partner. Take turns talking about your favorite places. Don't say
the places. Can your partner guess?

A This place has *lots of shops*, and there's
a video arcade. I go there to *hang out
with friends*. It's a great place
to *shop for clothes*.

B Hmm. Is it a *shopping mall*?

A Yeah, that's right. It's *City Center Mall*.

Talking about activities

I go there to It's a great place to When I'm there, I	hang out with friends. shop for clothes. play video games.

Organization focus

1 Josh's favorite place

A Look at the picture of Josh's favorite place. Where do you think it is? Why do you think it's his favorite place?

B Read Josh's brainstorming notes for his presentation about his favorite place. Check (✓) the seven topics he included in his outline on page 25.

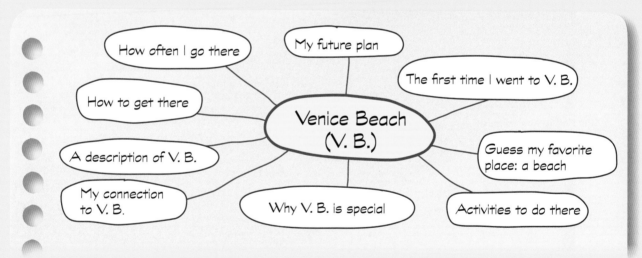

How often I go there

My future plan

The first time I went to V. B.

How to get there

Venice Beach (V. B.)

A description of V. B.

Guess my favorite place: a beach

My connection to V. B.

Why V. B. is special

Activities to do there

C Read Josh's additional notes for his presentation. Then use his notes to complete the outline on page 25.

- these days only once or twice a year
- plan to take pictures, can imagine I'm there
- hometown L. A., a big city, so feel comfortable in busy, noisy places

- relax and watch people
- holds many memories, reminds me of growing up
- long, narrow boardwalk, small shops

2 Josh's outline

🔊 12 Listen to Josh's presentation. Check the notes you added from Exercise 1C on page 24.

Venice Beach

I. Introduction

   A. My connection to V. B.

      1. California has great weather, so like warm, sunny places

      2. _____

      3. birth sign is Pisces (the fish), happy near water

   B. Guess my favorite place: a beach (V. B.)

   C. How often I go there

      1. used to spend a lot of time there

      2. _____

II. Body

   A. A description of V. B.

      1. big, wide, lively, crowded

      2. _____

      3. lots of restaurants, can get pizza, hot dogs, sushi

   B. Activities to do there

      1. hang out with old friends, get exercise

      2. bodysurf, cycle, enjoy the sunshine

      3. _____

      4. visitors stay near beach, sunbathe, jog, play volleyball

III. Conclusion

   A. Why V. B. is special

      1. always feels like home

      2. _____

      3. always changing, my memories will never change

   B. My future plan: _____

Presentation focus

1 Introduction

A Notice the information Josh included in the introduction of his presentation on page 27.

> ▶ His connection to the place
>
>   *California has great weather, so I like . . .*   *Because I'm a Pisces, . . .*
>
> ▶ The name of the place
>
> ▶ How often he goes there

B 💿 13 Guess the missing words in Josh's introduction. Then listen and check your guesses.

2 Body

A Notice the information Josh included in the body of his presentation on page 27.

> ▶ A description of the place
>
> ▶ Activities to do there

B 💿 14 Guess the missing words in the body of Josh's presentation. Then listen and check your guesses.

3 Conclusion

A Notice the information Josh included in the conclusion of his presentation on page 27.

> ▶ Why the place is special
>
>   *I like / love (place) because . . .*   *It's special to me because . . .*
>
> ▶ His future plan
>
>   *In the future, I plan to . . .*   *The next time I go there, . . .*

B 💿 15 Guess the missing words in Josh's conclusion. Then listen and check your guesses.

Venice Beach

Introduction

I'm from California. California has great weather, so I like warm, sunny places. My hometown is Los Angeles, and L. A. is a big city, so I feel comfortable in busy, noisy places. I was born in the month of March, and my _____ sign is Pisces, which means "the fish." Because I'm a Pisces, I'm happy near water. Perhaps now you can guess my favorite place. It's a beach! In fact, it's Venice Beach in L. A. I used to spend a lot of time there, but these _____ I only go there once or _____ a year.

Body

Venice Beach is a big, wide city beach. _____ always lively and crowded. It _____ a long, narrow boardwalk next to the sand. There _____ small shops that sell everything you can imagine — sunglasses, T-shirts, jewelry made of tiny seashells — all sorts of things. _____ are also lots of restaurants. You can get pizza, hot dogs, and even sushi! I go _____ to hang out with old friends or to get some exercise. _____ I'm there, I bodysurf, cycle along the boardwalk, and enjoy the sunshine. It's _____ great _____ to relax and watch people, too. Visitors can stay in hotels near the beach, sunbathe, jog, and play volleyball.

Conclusion

I love Venice Beach because it always _____ like home. It's special to me because it holds so many memories, and it reminds me of growing up in L. A. Venice Beach is always changing, but I know that my _____ will never change. In the future, I plan to take lots of pictures of Venice Beach. That way I can look at the pictures and imagine that I'm there, even when I'm far away.

Presentation skills focus

1 Gestures for describing size and shape

When you describe a place, use simple gestures to help the audience picture the scene.

Practice these gestures by yourself. Then practice with a partner. Say the sentences as you make the gestures.

> There's a **big** garden.

> It's **tall**.

> There are **long** benches.

> It's **small**.

> It has a **square** window.

Presentation tip
Don't be afraid to exaggerate your gestures. Make them slowly and clearly!

2 Your turn

A Write five sentences to describe a place you know well. Use words from the box.

Words to describe size and shape					
giant	large	narrow	round	square	thin
huge	little	oval	short	thick	tiny

1. It's _____ .

2. It has _____ .

3. There's _____ .

4. There are _____ .

5. _____

B Work with a partner. Read your sentences from Exercise A aloud. Use gestures to describe size and shape. Then ask your partner which gestures were most effective.

C Read the example from a presentation about a favorite place. Underline the words that describe size and shape.

> Sam's Books is a wonderful bookstore. It's very peaceful and quiet, and it has huge shelves full of books about all kinds of topics. I love to walk through the narrow rows between the shelves and look at all the interesting books. On the second floor, there are long sofas where people can relax. Sometimes I go there to enjoy a good book, and other times I go to do my English homework. Sam's has a large, oval table where I can spread out my things, and there's a big English dictionary that I can use to look up new vocabulary words.

D Take turns reading the example in Exercise C aloud. Practice gestures for describing size and shape.

Now present yourself!

- **Turn to page 30.**
- **Prepare your presentation.**

Present yourself! Give a presentation about a favorite place.

1 Brainstorming

Choose one of your favorite places. Write it in the center of the brainstorming map. Then add as many details as you can for each brainstorming topic.

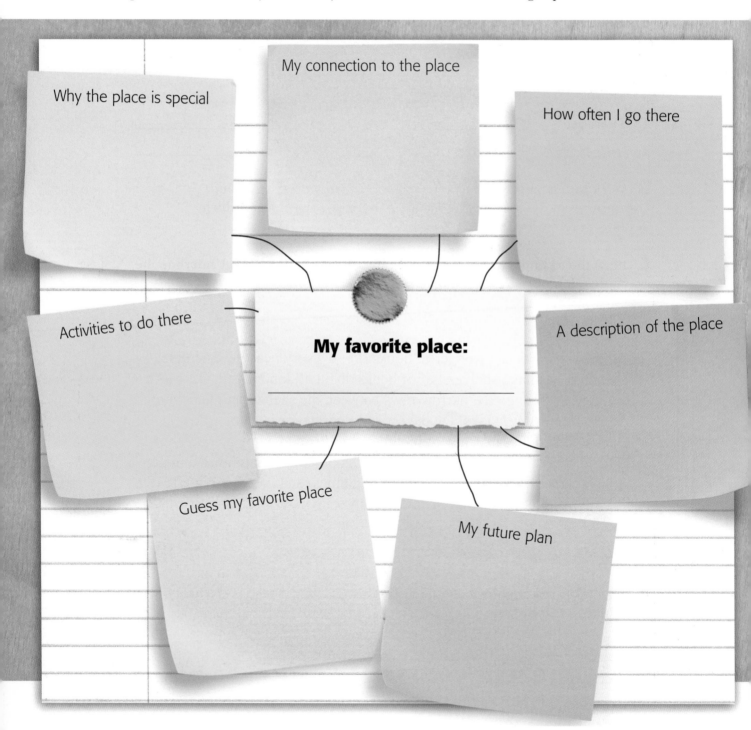

Why the place is special

My connection to the place

How often I go there

Activities to do there

My favorite place:

_____

A description of the place

Guess my favorite place

My future plan

2 Organizing

Use your brainstorming notes from Exercise 1 to complete the outline.
Then make note cards from your outline and practice your presentation.

_____
(title)

I.   Introduction

    A. My connection to the place

    _____

    B. Guess my favorite place

    _____

    C. How often I go there

    _____

II.   Body

    A. A description of the place

    _____

    B. Activities to do there

    _____

    _____

III. Conclusion

    A. Why the place is special

    _____

    B. My future plan

    _____

3 Presenting

Give your presentation to the class. Remember
to use gestures for describing size and shape.

Don't forget to complete
your self-evaluation on
page 81 after your presentation.

3 A prized possession

1 Possessions

A Why do you think these possessions are important to some people? Complete the chart with these possessions. Then add one more to each category.

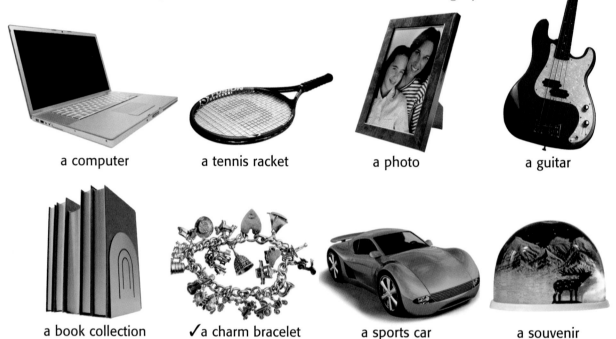

a computer a tennis racket a photo a guitar

a book collection ✓a charm bracelet a sports car a souvenir

brings good luck	helps save time	makes life more fun
a charm bracelet		

brings back memories	helps relieve stress	makes life more meaningful

B Work with a partner. Compare your charts in Exercise A.

A What do you think *brings good luck*?

B I think *a charm bracelet brings good luck*. How about you?

A I agree. A coin *brings good luck*, too.

2 Possessions survey

A Complete the survey. Ask your classmates questions.

"What's something that . . . ?"
   "Why is it important to you?"

What's something that . . . ?	Classmate	Possession	Reason it's important
you've had for a long time	Yumi	a silver necklace	brings back memories of her grandmother
you use every day			
you would never lend to anybody			
you take with you everywhere			
you would be very sad to lose			
was a gift from someone			

B Tell the class about some of your classmates' possessions.

"Yumi has a silver necklace. It brings back memories of her grandmother."

3 My prized possessions

A Complete the chart with information about two of your prized possessions.

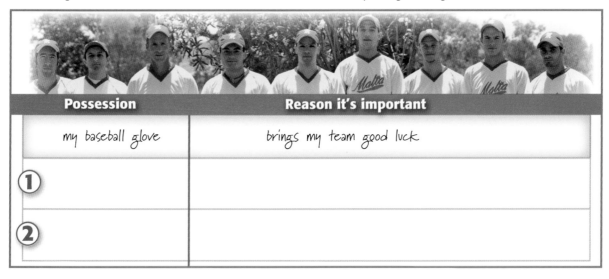

Possession	Reason it's important
my baseball glove	brings my team good luck
①	
②	

B Tell a partner about your two prized possessions.

"My baseball glove is important to me because it brings my team good luck."

Language focus

1 **What does it look like?**

A 🔘 16   Listen to Mei, Lisa, and Greg describe their possessions. Number the possessions from 1 to 3. (There are five extra possessions.)

B Complete the chart with words from the box.

Words to describe possessions

✓checked	faded	rectangular	round	striped	tiny
denim	plastic	rough	smooth	thick	torn

Size	Shape	Texture

Pattern	Material	Condition
checked		

C Take turns describing the objects in Exercise A. Don't say them. Can your partner guess?

A It's *small* and *round*. It has *flowers* on it, and it's made of *gold*.

B Is it the *watch*?

A Yes! You're right.
         or
Sorry! Guess again.

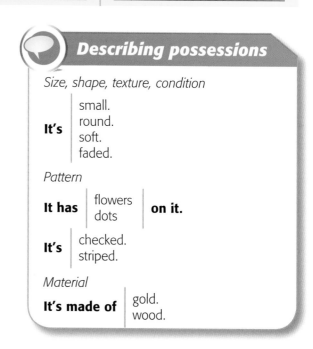

💬 **Describing possessions**

Size, shape, texture, condition

It's | small.
          | round.
          | soft.
          | faded.

Pattern

It has | flowers | **on it.**
           | dots

It's | checked.
         | striped.

Material

It's made of | gold.
                 | wood.

2) Here's the history.

A 🔘 17   Now listen to Mei, Lisa, and Greg describe the history of their possessions. Circle the correct information.

	Where I got it	**How long I've had it**	**How I use it**
1. Mei	as a *gift* / *souvenir*	for five *months* / *years*	when I *work* / *relax*
2. Lisa	from my *friend* / *parents*	since *high school* / *university*	to keep *memories* / *photos*
3. Greg	in *Italy* / *Greece*	since last *fall* / *summer*	to drink *coffee* / *tea*

B   Complete the chart with information about two of your prized possessions.

Possession	Where I got it	How long I've had it	How I use it
my baseball glove	as a birthday gift	for six years	when I play baseball every Saturday
1.			
2.			

C   Work with a partner. Take turns explaining the history of your possessions from Exercise B.

A   One of my favorite possessions is *my baseball glove*. I got it *as a birthday gift*.

B   How long have you had it?

A   I've had it *for six years*. I use it *when I play baseball every Saturday*.

Explaining the history

It was a	birthday graduation	**gift.**

I got it	as a gift. from my teacher. in Taipei.		

I've had it	**for**	six a few	**years.**
	since	1995. high school.	

I use it	**when I** play baseball. **to** keep photos.

Organization focus

1 Ann's prized possession

A Look at the picture of Ann's prized possession. Describe it with a partner. Why do you think it's important to Ann?

B Read Ann's brainstorming notes for her presentation about her prized possession. Check (✔) the eight topics she included in her outline on page 37.

My Mini Zen Garden

Reasons why it's important
How I use it
Why the possession is special
How much it cost
Why I need the possession

The history of it
What the possession is
A wish for the future
A description of the possession

C Read Ann's additional notes for her presentation. Then use her notes to complete the outline on page 37.

- plan to keep it for a long time
- sometimes feel stressed, need time to relax
- gift from a stranger

- makes life more meaningful
- has light brown sand, gray stones inside it
- use it when I want to feel calm

2 Ann's outline

18 Listen to Ann's presentation. Check the notes you added from Exercise 1C on page 36.

My Mini Zen Garden

I.   Introduction
   A. Why I need the possession
      1. always busy because I go to school, have a part-time job
      2. _____
   B. Reasons why it's important
      1. helps relieve stress
      2. _____
   C. What the possession is: my mini Zen garden

II. Body
   A. A description of the possession
      1. small, rectangular
      2. made of wood
      3. _____
   B. The history of it
      1. had it for about three years
      2. _____
   C. How I use it
      1. look at it when I need to relax
      2. _____

III. Conclusion
   A. Why the possession is special
      1. keeps my mind and heart calm
      2. reminds me that simple things are best
   B. A wish for the future
      1. _____
      2. hope to carry the spirit of my garden inside me

Presentation focus

1 Introduction

A Notice the information Ann included in the introduction of her presentation on page 39.

> ▶ Why she needs the possession
>   *I'm always busy because . . .*   *Sometimes I feel . . .*
>
> ▶ Reasons why it's important
>
> ▶ What the possession is
>   *Here it is: my . . .*

B 💿 19   Guess the missing words in Ann's introduction. Then listen and check your guesses.

2 Body

A Notice the information Ann included in the body of her presentation on page 39.

> ▶ A description of the possession
>
> ▶ The history of it
>
> ▶ How she uses it

B 💿 20   Guess the missing words in the body of Ann's presentation. Then listen and check your guesses.

3 Conclusion

A Notice the information Ann included in the conclusion of her presentation on page 39.

> ▶ Why the possession is special
>   *It's special to me for many reasons.*   *It reminds me that . . .*
>
> ▶ A wish for the future
>   *In the future, I hope / plan to . . .*

B 💿 21   Guess the missing words in Ann's conclusion. Then listen and check your guesses.

My Mini Zen Garden

I'm always busy because I go to school and I have a part-time job, too. Sometimes I feel stressed, and I need time to relax. There are many ways to deal with stress, for example, taking yoga classes or going on vacation, but those things can be expensive, and I don't have a lot of money. My prized possession didn't cost any money at all. It's important to me because it really helps _____ stress. It's also important because it _____ my life _____ meaningful. I'd like to share my prized possession with you today. Here it is: my mini Zen garden!

Body

As you can see, _____ small and rectangular. And here on the bottom, it's _____ of wood. It _____ light brown sand and gray stones inside it. I've had my Zen garden _____ about three years. I got it as a _____ when I started at the university. In fact, it was a gift from a stranger. In my new dorm room, I saw a small, brown box on the bookshelf. There was a note on the box that said, "To the next student who lives in this room. Please enjoy this!" I opened the box, and this Zen garden was inside it. I was amazed! These days, I look at my Zen garden _____ I need to relax, and I use it _____ I want to feel calm. Every Sunday morning, I make a new pattern in the sand.

Conclusion

My Zen garden is special to me for many reasons. It keeps my mind and _____ calm when my life is full of stress, and it reminds me that the _____ things in life are the best. I plan to keep my garden for a long time – wherever I live and whatever I do. In the future, I hope to carry the spirit of my garden inside me.

1 Show-and-tell expressions

When you present your possession, show it to the audience and point out its features.

Match the sentences to the pictures. (There is one extra sentence.)

a. As you can see, it's striped.
b. Can you all see that it's faded?
c. Here on the bottom, there's a patch.
d. Here on the top, it's smooth.
e. Here on the back, there's a camera.

Presentation tip

Follow these steps when you present an object to an audience:
1. Keep your possession hidden until the end of your introduction.
2. Then take it out, hold it up, and show it to the audience for a few seconds.
3. Put your possession down where the audience can see it.
4. Hold it up again when you point out certain features.

2 | Your turn

A Choose a possession you have with you now. Write it below. Then write four sentences to describe its features. Use language from the box.

> ### Show-and-tell expressions
>
> | As you can see, . . . Can you all see that . . . | Here on the | top . . . bottom . . . front . . . back . . . |
> | --- | --- | --- |

My possession: _____

1. _____
2. _____
3. _____
4. _____

B Work in groups. Take turns showing and describing your possessions from Exercise A.

"This is my book bag. As you can see, . . . "

C Read the example from a presentation about a prized possession. Underline the show-and-tell expressions.

I'd like to share my prized possession with you today. Here it is . . . my photo album. As you can see, it's really big and thick, and it has lots of pictures in it. The cover is made of smooth, brown leather. Here on the front, it has little flowers around the edge. And can you all see that it has my name and my birth date printed on it? I got this photo album as a gift from my mother when I turned 18. It has pictures of me from the day I was born and all through my childhood.

D Take turns reading the example in Exercise C aloud. Hold up a notebook and imagine you are showing the photo album. Practice show-and-tell expressions.

Now **present yourself!**

- **Turn to page 42.**
- **Prepare your presentation.**

Present yourself!

Give a presentation about one of your prized possessions.

1 Brainstorming

Choose one of your prized possessions. Write it at the top of the brainstorming map. Then add as many details as you can for each brainstorming topic.

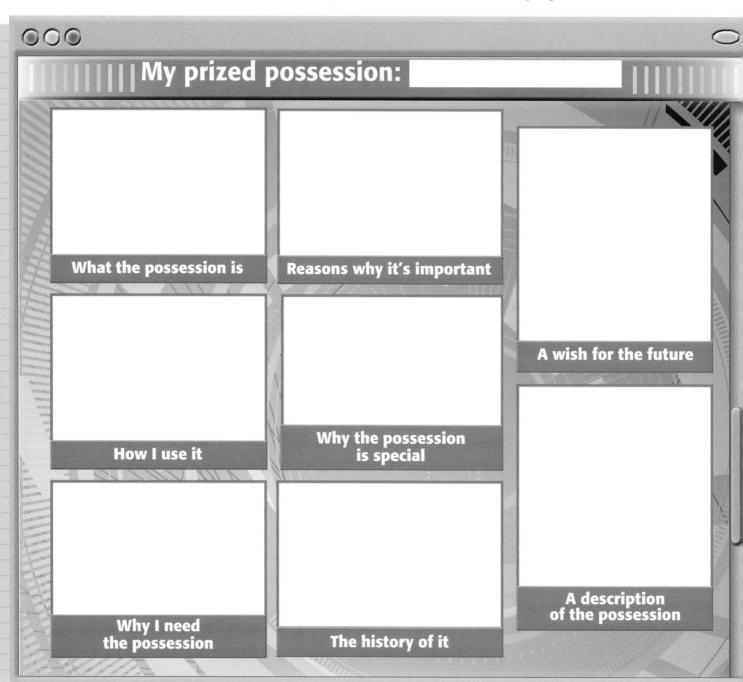

My prized possession: _____

What the possession is

Reasons why it's important

A wish for the future

How I use it

Why the possession is special

Why I need the possession

The history of it

A description of the possession

2 Organizing

Use your brainstorming notes from Exercise 1 to complete the outline.
Then make note cards from your outline and practice your presentation.

_____
(title)

I.   Introduction

   A. Why I need the possession

   _____

   B. Reasons why it's important

   _____

   C. What the possession is

   _____

II. Body

   A. A description of the possession

   _____

   B. The history of it

   _____

   C. How I use it

   _____

   _____

III. Conclusion

   A. Why the possession is special

   _____

   B. A wish for the future

   _____

3 Presenting

Give your presentation to the class.
Remember to use show-and-tell expressions.

Don't forget to complete
your self-evaluation on
page 82 after your presentation.

4 A memorable experience

Topic focus

1 Experiences

A Match the sentences to the pictures. (There are two extra sentences.)

a. I was very surprised.   c. It was so amazing!   e. It was really frustrating!

b. It was so scary!   d. I was really bored.   f. I was very embarrassed.

1.

2.

3.

4.

B Do these words describe experiences or feelings? Complete the chart. Then add more words to each column.

Words to describe experiences and feelings					
✓ shocking	surprising	exciting	scared	shocked	boring
interesting	frustrated	amazed	interested	excited	embarrassing

Describing experiences	Describing feelings
It was *really / so / very* . . . shocking	I was *really / so / very* . . .

C Have you had experiences like the ones in Exercise A? Tell a partner about the experiences and your feelings.

"I saw my favorite band in concert last year. It was really exciting. I was so amazed."

2 An experience when . . .

A Check (✓) the experiences you have had. Then complete the chart with information about your experiences.

An experience when I . . .	When	The experience / My feelings
✓ did something for the first time ___learned how to drive___	last summer	very scary, really excited
☐ won an award _____		
☐ achieved something difficult _____		
☐ did something I regretted _____		
☐ lost or found something _____		
☐ made an important decision _____		
☐ had good luck _____		

B Work with a partner. Take turns asking each other about the experiences in Exercise A. Take notes on a separate piece of paper.

A Jun Ho, can you tell me about an experience when you *did something for the first time?*

B Yes. I *learned how to drive last summer.*

A Oh, what was it like?

B It was *very scary*, but I was *really excited.*

C Join another pair of students. Tell them about some of your partner's experiences.

"Jun Ho learned how to drive last summer. It was very scary, but he was really excited."

Language focus

1 Setting the scene

A 💿 22 Listen to Tina, John, and Naomi talk about their experiences. Number the pictures from 1 to 3. (There is one extra picture.)

B 💿 22 Listen again. When and where did they have the experiences? Circle the correct information.

	1. Tina	**2. John**	**3. Naomi**
When	a few *months / years* ago	last *spring / winter*	*exactly / almost* one year ago
Where	at a *café / restaurant*	in *Spain / Switzerland*	in *Canada / Hawaii*

C Work with a partner. Take turns talking about these experiences.

> **An experience when you . . .**
>
> made a new friend   saw something amazing   had bad luck   did something exciting

A Tell me about an experience when you *made a new friend*.

B Well, this happened to me *in 1996*. I was *in Europe*. I went to *the beach*, and I . . .

Setting the scene

When

This happened to me **I had this experience**	in 1996. in high school. a few years ago. last summer.

Where
I was in Europe.
I went to the beach.
It happened at my office.

2 Telling the story

A 🔘 23 Now listen to Tina, John, and Naomi tell their stories. Number the sentences in the correct order from 1 to 4.

1. Tina
   - [3] He sat next to us.
   - [1] I went out for lunch.
   - [2] I saw Jim Thomas.
   - [4] He gave us concert tickets.

2. John
   - [ ] I took a lesson.
   - [ ] I improved a little.
   - [ ] I fell a lot.
   - [ ] I learned to jump.

3. Naomi
   - [ ] I didn't want to go home.
   - [ ] I couldn't communicate.
   - [ ] I learned more English.
   - [ ] My host family greeted me.

B 🔘 23 Listen again. Which time expressions do they use in the beginning, middle, and end of their stories? Write *T* (Tina), *J* (John), or *N* (Naomi) next to the expressions.

Time expressions		
Beginning	**Middle**	**End**
____ at first	____ after a while	____ by the end
____ in the beginning	____ later on	____ finally
____ one day	____ suddenly	____ in the end

C Work with a partner. Take turns telling Tina, John, and Naomi's stories in your own words.

"One day, Tina went out for lunch. Suddenly, she saw . . . "

3 My experience

Complete the chart with information about a memorable experience. Then tell the class about your experience.

When and where	What happened
• had this experience a few years ago • went to Australia	• took a scuba diving tour • saw three dolphins • one dolphin came and swam near me • touched it

"I had this experience a few years ago. I went to Australia. One day, I took a scuba diving tour. Suddenly, I saw . . . "

Organization focus

1 Alex's memorable experience

A Look at the picture of Alex's memorable experience. What was the experience? How do you think he felt?

B Read Alex's brainstorming notes for his presentation about his memorable experience. Check (✓) the seven topics he included in his outline on page 49.

My Sailing Trip

What happened   A question to introduce the topic

A description of the experience and   When and where I had the experience

my feelings   How I felt after the experience

Where I want to go next   What the experience was

What I learned

C Read Alex's additional notes for his presentation. Then use his notes to complete the outline on page 49.

- learned about other places, cultures   • weather changed, we were in storm

- never bored   • when it was over, really sad

- storm ended, had smooth seas, visited   • last summer
  small islands

- three-week sailing trip

2 Alex's outline

🔘 24   Listen to Alex's presentation. Check the notes you added from Exercise 1C on page 48.

My Sailing Trip

I. Introduction

    A.   A question to introduce the topic: How many of you have been abroad?

    B.   What the experience was

        1. _____

        2. went on friend Tom's sailboat

    C.   A description of the experience and my feelings

        1. really amazing, very scary

        2. _____

II. Body

    A.   When and where I had the experience

        1. several countries in South Pacific Ocean

        2. _____

    B.   What happened

        1. The beginning

            a. left Hong Kong, headed toward the Philippines

            b. sea was calm

        2. The middle

            a. _____

            b. got used to waves, boat moving

            c. _____

        3. The end

            a. saw skyscrapers of Singapore

            b. couldn't believe we had arrived at our destination

III. Conclusion

    A.   How I felt after the experience

        1. _____

        2. thankful to have had that wonderful opportunity

    B.   What I learned

        1. _____

        2. made me realize there's another world out there

Presentation focus

1 Introduction

A Notice the information Alex included in the introduction of his presentation on page 51.

> ▶ A question to introduce the topic
>
> *How many of you have . . . ?*   *Have you ever . . . ?*
>
> ▶ What the experience was
>
> ▶ A description of the experience and his feelings

B 🔘 25   Guess the missing words in Alex's introduction. Then listen and check your guesses.

2 Body

A Notice the information Alex included in the body of his presentation on page 51.

> ▶ When and where he had the experience (setting the scene)
>
> ▶ What happened

B 🔘 26   Guess the missing words in the body of Alex's presentation. Then listen and check your guesses.

3 Conclusion

A Notice the information Alex included in the conclusion of his presentation on page 51.

> ▶ How he felt after the experience
>
> *When the trip was over, I was . . .*
>
> ▶ What he learned
>
> *I learned a lot about . . .*   *This experience made me realize . . .*

B 🔘 27   Guess the missing words in Alex's conclusion. Then listen and check your guesses.

My Sailing Trip

Introduction

How many of you have been abroad? A lot of you, right? But have you ever traveled by sailboat? Well, I was lucky enough to have that experience. Now I'm going to tell you all about my trip – a three-week _____ trip. I went with my friend Tom and his family on their sailboat. The trip was really amazing. _____ was very scary at times, but those moments made it even more exciting. _____ was never bored, not even for a minute.

Body

I had this _____ last summer. We went to several countries in the South Pacific Ocean. On the first day, we left Hong Kong, and headed south toward the Philippines. In the _____ , the sea was calm. But _____ , the weather changed, and we were in a big storm! I was so frightened at first, but after a _____ , I got used to the big waves and the boat moving from side to side. Later _____ , the storm ended, and we had smooth seas for the rest of the trip. We sailed around the Philippines and visited small islands for about a week. It was really interesting. _____ , we saw the skyscrapers of Singapore. I couldn't believe it. We had arrived at our final destination.

Conclusion

When the trip was over, I was really sad because I didn't want my experience to end. But I was so thankful to have had that _____ opportunity. I learned a lot about other places and cultures. This experience made me realize that there's another _____ out there. And it's waiting for you, too. Thank you.

Presentation skills focus

1 Using stress and emphasis with *really*, *so*, and *very*

Use the intensifiers *really*, *so*, and *very* to create a dramatic effect when you describe experiences and feelings.

A 🔘 28 Listen. Notice the intensifiers. Then listen again and repeat the sentences.

I was **really** embarrassed.

1

I was **so** shocked!

2

I was **very** bored.

3

The storm was **really** scary!

4

The concert was **so** exciting!

5

It was **very** frustrating.

6

B 🔘 29 Listen to more people describe experiences and feelings. Complete the sentences.

1. When the summer was over, I was _____ sad.

2. I visited China last year. It was _____ interesting.

3. The baseball game was _____ amazing! My team won!

4. I tried bungee jumping once. I was _____ scared!

5. I was roller-skating and I fell down. It was _____ embarrassing.

Presentation tip

To create even more dramatic effect, say the intensifiers more slowly than the rest of the sentence.

2 Your turn

A Choose an experience from the box. Write it below. Then complete the information about the experience. Use intensifiers.

> a crazy adventure   a fun night out
> a dangerous event   a great concert or show

The experience: _____

When and where the experience happened: _____

Sentences about the experience:

1. _____
2. _____
3. _____
4. _____

B Work with a partner. Take turns describing your experiences from Exercise A.

"I'm going to tell you about a fun night out. I had this experience last weekend. I went to a party. It was . . . "

C Read the example from a presentation about a memorable experience. Underline the intensifiers.

> I'm going to tell you about a scary adventure. This happened to me a few years ago. I went to my aunt's house in the country to spend the summer. At first, I was really bored because there wasn't anything to do, but after a while, I enjoyed being in the country. One day, I took a walk in the woods. It was very peaceful and quiet. Suddenly, I heard something behind me. I turned around and saw a huge black bear. I was so frightened. I ran out of the woods as fast as I could. I'll never forget that experience. I was very scared, but it was really exciting.

D Take turns reading the example in Exercise C aloud. Practice using intensifiers with stress and emphasis.

Now **present yourself!**

- **Turn to page 54.**
- **Prepare your presentation.**

Present yourself! Give a presentation about a memorable experience.

1 Brainstorming

Choose one of your memorable experiences. Write it in the center of the brainstorming map. Then add as many details as you can for each brainstorming topic.

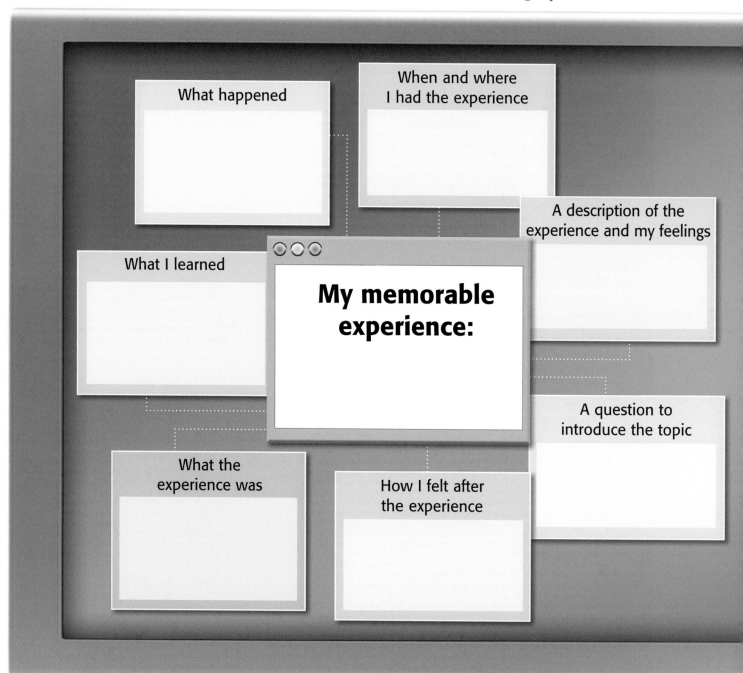

What happened

When and where I had the experience

A description of the experience and my feelings

What I learned

My memorable experience:

What the experience was

How I felt after the experience

A question to introduce the topic

2 Organizing

Use your brainstorming notes from Exercise 1 to complete the outline.
Then make note cards from your outline and practice your presentation.

_____
(title)

I. Introduction

    A. A question to introduce the topic

    _____

    B. What the experience was

    _____

    _____

    C. A description of the experience and my feelings

    _____

II. Body

    A. When and where I had the experience

    _____

    B. What happened

    _____

    _____

III. Conclusion

    A. How I felt after the experience

    _____

    B. What I learned

    _____

3 Presenting

Give your presentation to the class. Remember
to use the intensifiers *really*, *so*, and *very*.

Don't forget to complete
your self-evaluation on
page 83 after your presentation.

5 Show me how.

Topic focus

1 Skills and talents

A How many skills and talents can you think of? Write them in the chart.

Skills and Talents

Art
make pottery
_____
_____
_____

Music
play the flute
_____
_____
_____

Clothing and fashion
knit scarves
_____
_____
_____

Performing
juggle
_____
_____
_____

Computers and technology
play computer games
_____
_____
_____

Sports and fitness
do yoga
_____
_____
_____

Cooking
bake cakes
_____
_____
_____

Traditional crafts
do origami
_____
_____
_____

B Why is it useful to know these skills and talents? Read the reasons.
Then compare ideas with a partner.

You can . . .		It can . . .	
decorate your home	entertain people	help with your work	improve your health
earn or save money	make gifts for people	help you relax	make studying easier

"It's useful to know how to make pottery because you can make gifts for people."
    "Yes, and it can help you relax, too."

2 | Talent search

A Complete the survey. Ask your classmates questions.

"Do you know how to make your own greeting cards?"
     "Why do you think it's useful?"

Do you know how to . . . ?	Classmate	Reason it's useful
make your own greeting cards	Eva	can save a lot of money
do a fitness exercise at home		
create a Web page		
sew or knit your own clothes		
prepare a tasty dish		
make an origami animal		
play a musical instrument		
learn English vocabulary easily		

B Tell the class about some of your classmates' skills and talents.

"Eva makes her own greeting cards. It's useful because . . . "

3 | My talents

A Complete the chart with information about two of your skills or talents.

Skill or talent	Reason it's useful
knit scarves	can help you relax
❶	
❷	

B Tell a partner about your skills and talents.

"I know how to knit scarves. It's useful because it can help you relax, and . . . "

Language focus

1 Here's what you need.

A 🔘 30 Listen to Mark, Tomo, and Rob introduce their demonstrations. Number the demonstrations from 1 to 3. (There is one extra demonstration.)

TODAY'S DEMONSTRATIONS

Tips for
Keeping Fit
9:30 – 10:30 a.m.
☐

Build
a Birdhouse
1:00 – 2:00 p.m.
☐

Quick Snacks
2:30 – 3:30 p.m.
☐

Easy Tricks
4:00 – 5:00 p.m.
☐

B 🔘 31 Now listen to them present the materials they need for their demonstrations. Write *M* (Mark), *T* (Tomo), or *R* (Rob) next to the three things they need.

_____ two avocados	_____ a glass bottle	_____ a mat
_____ a box of matches	_____ a hard-boiled egg	_____ an onion
_____ a chair	_____ a jar of paint	_____ a hammer
_____ pieces of wood	_____ loose clothing	_____ a tomato

C Choose two demonstrations from the box. Then write three things you need for each demonstration on a separate piece of paper.

How to . . .		
boil an egg	make a greeting card	make a milkshake
make a cup of tea	make an ice-cream sundae	wrap a gift

D Work in groups. Take turns presenting the things you need. Don't name the demonstrations. Who can guess first?

A Before you begin, you need
a pot, . . .

B I know! It's, *"How to boil an egg."*

A Yes! You're right.
      or
Sorry! Guess again.

Presenting the materials you need

Before you begin, you need **Here's what you need to start:** **For this, you should have**	a pot, an egg, and some water.

2 Follow the steps.

A 🔘 32   What are the instructions for Rob's demonstration? Number the pictures in order from 1 to 6. Then listen and check your guesses.

☐ Light the matches.

☐ Put the egg on the bottle.

☐ Boil and peel the egg.

☐ Put the matches in the bottle.

☐ Watch the egg go inside.

☐ Let the matches burn out.

B   Think of a simple snack or drink you know how to make. Write the instructions on a separate piece of paper.

How to make a grilled cheese sandwich
1. Slice the cheese.
2. Put the cheese on the bread.
3. Put the bread in the pan . . .

> **Giving instructions**
>
> **First,** slice the cheese.
> **Next,** put the cheese on the bread.
> **Then,** put the bread in the pan.
> **After that,** wait until the cheese melts.
> **Finally,** take it out of the pan and eat it.
> **There are** three **more steps to go.**
> **We're almost finished.**
> **We're halfway there.**

C   Work with a partner. Take turns giving your instructions.

*"I'm going to tell you how to make a grilled cheese sandwich.
First, slice the cheese. Next, put the cheese on the bread. OK. There
are three more steps to go . . ."*

Organization focus

1 Maria's demonstration

A Look at the steps of Maria's demonstration. What is she demonstrating? What do you think her instructions are?

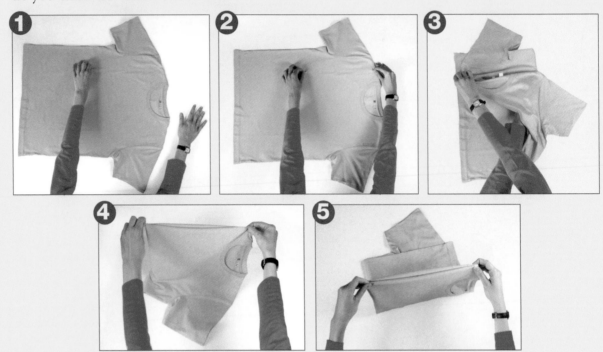

B Read Maria's brainstorming notes for her demonstration. Check (✓) the seven topics she included in her outline on page 61.

How to Fold a T-shirt

Reasons why the skill is useful to know
The materials you need
The audience's needs and interests
The instructions

The number of steps
How I learned the skill
The topic of my demonstration
How the skill will help the audience in the future

C Read Maria's additional notes for her demonstration. Then use her notes to complete the outline on page 61.

- how to fold a T-shirt
- lay T-shirt down and fold it over sleeve
- don't have time to do chores
- next time you pack, able to take more shirts

- two steps to go
- should have a clean, flat space
- can keep shirts looking neat

2 Maria's outline

🔘 33   Listen to Maria's demonstration. Check the notes you added from Exercise 1C on Page 60.

How to Fold a T-shirt

I.   Introduction

A. The audience's needs and interests

1. all busy students

2. _____

B. The topic of my demonstration: _____

C. Reasons why the skill is useful to know

1. can save you lots of time

2. _____

II. Body

A. The materials you need

1. T-shirt or short-sleeved shirt

2. _____

B. The instructions

1. pinch T-shirt halfway down with left hand

2. pinch T-shirt at top between neck and shoulder with right hand

3. cross right hand over left hand, pinch bottom of T-shirt with right hand

4. _____

a. uncross arms, straighten T-shirt

b. _____

III. Conclusion

A. The number of steps: five

B. How the skill will help the audience in the future

1. can save space in your shirt drawer

2. _____

Presentation focus

1 Introduction

A Notice the information Maria included in the introduction of her demonstration on page 63.

► The audience's needs and interests
You're all busy . . .   You don't have much time to . . .

► The topic of her demonstration
Today I'm going to show you . . .

► Reasons why the skill is useful to know

B 34 Guess the missing words in Maria's introduction. Then listen and check your guesses.

2 Body

A Notice the information Maria included in the body of her demonstration on page 63.

► The materials you need

► The instructions

B 35 Guess the missing words in the body of Maria's demonstration. Then listen and check your guesses.

3 Conclusion

A Notice the information Maria included in the conclusion of her demonstration on page 63.

► The number of steps

► How the skill will help the audience in the future
The next time you . . .   Whenever you need to . . .

B 36 Guess the missing words in Maria's conclusion. Then listen and check your guesses.

How to Fold a T-shirt

Good afternoon, everyone. You're all busy students, and I know you don't have much time to do chores at home. However, everybody has to put away clothes after they're washed, right? Well, today I'm going to show you how to _____ a T-shirt. You'll be able to fold all your shirts this way, simply and quickly. It _____ save you lots of time, and you _____ keep your shirts looking neat.

OK, let's get started. Before you _____ , you need a T-shirt or a short-sleeved shirt. And for this, you _____ have a clean, flat space to lay the T-shirt down, front facing up. Make sure the neck of the T-shirt is facing sideways, on your right. Here's how you do it. _____ , with your left hand, pinch the T-shirt halfway down from the neck and about five centimeters from the side that is farthest from you. Next, with your right hand, pinch the T-shirt at the very top between the neck and the shoulder, on the side that is farthest from you. Your hands should form a straight line. Is that part clear? All right. Then, cross your right hand over your left hand and, after _____ , with your right hand, also pinch the very bottom of the T-shirt. Be sure to keep your left hand pinching the middle. Are there any questions? . . . No? Great. There are only two more _____ to go! Next, with both hands still pinching the T-shirt, uncross your arms and straighten the T-shirt up in front of you, like this! _____ , lay the T-shirt face down and fold it over the sleeve, and you've done it!

So, that's how to fold a T-shirt in five simple steps. Remember the five _____ , and you'll do it easily every time. I'm sure you'll be glad you learned this skill. It can save space in your _____ drawer. And the next time you pack for a vacation, you'll be able to take so many more shirts! Thank you!

Presentation skills focus

1 Emphasizing key points

During your demonstration, emphasize key points to help keep the audience focused.

Match the key points to the pictures. (There is one extra key point.)

a. Don't forget to turn on the oven timer.
b. Be sure to cut the right size.
c. Remember to save your work.
d. It's important to wear loose clothing.
e. Be sure to start with the wide end longer.

1.

2.

3.

4.

Presentation tip

Follow these steps for giving instructions effectively:
1. Emphasize key points.
2. Ask the audience if they understand.
      For example: *Are there any questions?*   *Is that part clear?*
3. Repeat any instructions that weren't clear.

2 Your turn

A Write one more key point for each demonstration on page 64.
Use language from the box.

> ### Emphasizing key points
>
> Remember to . . .   It's important to . . .
> Don't forget to . . .   Be sure to . . .

1. _____
2. _____
3. _____
4. _____

B Work with a partner. Take turns reading your key points from Exercise A. Don't name the demonstrations. Don't say them in order. Can your partner guess?

"Remember to add the baking powder."
  "I know! It's, 'How to Bake a Cake.'"

C Read the example from a demonstration. Underline the sentences that emphasize key points.

Here's what you need to start: a box, some gift paper, some scissors, some tape, and a
bow. First, cut a piece of paper. Be sure to cut the right size – not too big and not too
small. Next, put the box on the paper. It's important to put it right in the middle. Then, fold
the sides up and over the top of the box. Remember to smooth out any wrinkles in the
paper. Are there any questions? After that, tape the two sides together. Then, fold the
ends in carefully, like this. Is that part clear? Great. Finally, fold the end pieces up and put
on more tape. Oh, and don't forget to put the bow on the top.

D Take turns reading the example in Exercise C aloud. Practice emphasizing key points.

Now **present yourself!**

- **Turn to page 66.**
- **Prepare your presentation.**

Present yourself!

Demonstrate a skill or talent.

1 Brainstorming

Choose one of your skills or talents. Write it at the top of the brainstorming map. Then add as many details as you can for each brainstorming topic.

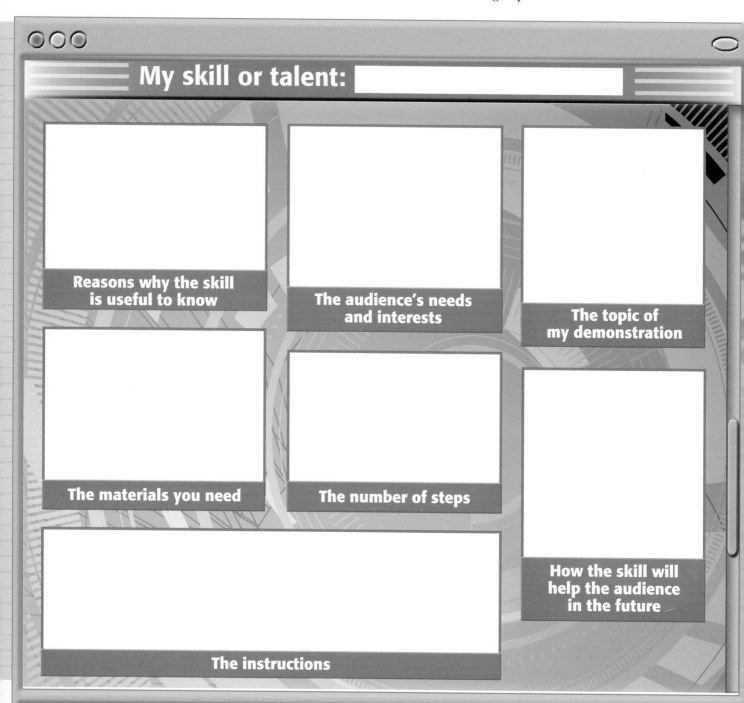

My skill or talent:

Reasons why the skill is useful to know

The audience's needs and interests

The topic of my demonstration

The materials you need

The number of steps

How the skill will help the audience in the future

The instructions

2 Organizing

Use your brainstorming notes from Exercise 1 to complete the outline.
Then make note cards from your outline and practice your presentation.

_____
(title)

I. Introduction

    A. The audience's needs and interests

    _____

    B. The topic of my demonstration

    _____

    C. Reasons why the skill is useful to know

    _____

II. Body

    A. The materials you need

    _____

    _____

    B. The instructions

    _____

    _____

III. Conclusion

    A. The number of steps

    _____

    B. How the skill will help the audience in the future

    _____

3 Presenting

Present your demonstration to the class.
Remember to emphasize key points.

Don't forget to complete
your self-evaluation on
page 84 after your presentation.

6 Movie magic

Topic focus

1 Movie quiz

A Circle your answers to the movie quiz. Then compare answers with a partner. (You can check your answers at the bottom of the quiz.)

Movie Quiz

1 Who said, "Life is like a box of chocolates. You never know what you're going to get."?

   a. Batman   b. Forrest Gump   c. Willy Wonka

2 Where are the most movies made every year?

   a. Hollywood   b. Shanghai   c. Mumbai

3 The first movie was shown in a theater about 110 years ago. Where?

   a. Paris   b. Hollywood   c. New York City

4 Which of these famous musicals is based on the play *Romeo and Juliet* by William Shakespeare?

   a. *The Sound of Music*   b. *Chicago*   c. *West Side Story*

5 What is the setting for the *Batman* movies?

   a. Gotham City   b. Los Angeles   c. London

6 Who was the director of *Titanic*, starring Leonardo DiCaprio?

   a. Steven Spielberg   b. James Cameron   c. Quentin Tarantino

7 Which martial arts expert starred in the *Rush Hour* action comedies?

   a. Jackie Chan   b. Jet Li   c. Steven Seagal

Quiz answers: 1. b; 2. c; 3. a; 4. c; 5. a; 6. b; 7. a

B Write two more movie quiz questions with answer choices on a separate piece of paper. Then ask your partner the questions.

"Who played Spider-Man? Was it Brad Pitt, Tobey Maguire, or George Clooney?"
      "I think it was Tobey Maguire."

2 Movie highlights

A Complete the chart with information about movies you know.

A movie that has . . .	Title	Lead actor	Setting (where, when)
an exciting battle scene	Gladiator	Russell Crowe	Rome, about 2,000 years ago
an amazing car chase			
a sad ending			
great special effects			
beautiful costumes			
a confusing story			

B Work with a partner. Take turns asking each other about the movies in Exercise A. Take notes on a separate piece of paper.

A What's a movie that has *an exciting battle scene*?

B *Gladiator.*

A Who's the lead actor?

B It stars *Russell Crowe.*

A What's the setting?

B It's set in *Rome, about two thousand years ago.*

C Tell the class about one of your partner's movies.

*"Gladiator **has an exciting battle scene. It stars . . . "**

3 My favorite movies

A Complete the chart with information about two of your favorite movies.

Movie title	Lead actor	Setting
Night at the Museum	Ben Stiller	New York City, today
1.		
2.		

B Tell your partner about your favorite movies.

*"One of my favorite movies is **Night at the Museum**. It stars Ben Stiller, and it's set in . . . "*

Language focus

1 What's it about?

A 🔊 37 What do you know about these movies? Check (✓) the information below. Then listen and check your guesses.

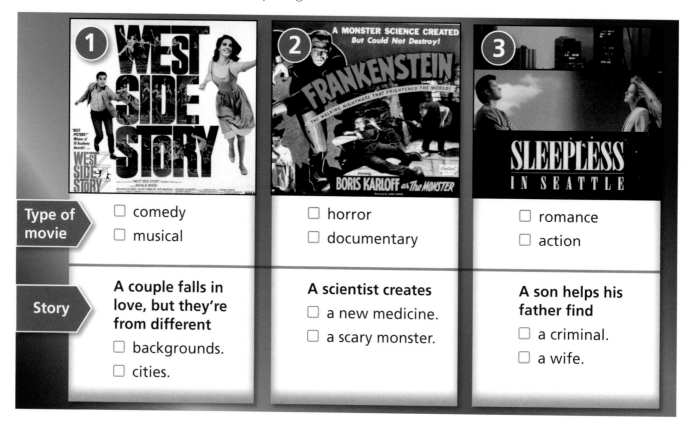

	① **WEST SIDE STORY**	② **FRANKENSTEIN** — A MONSTER SCIENCE CREATED But Could Not Destroy! — BORIS KARLOFF as The Monster	③ **SLEEPLESS IN SEATTLE**
Type of movie	☐ comedy ☐ musical	☐ horror ☐ documentary	☐ romance ☐ action
Story	A couple falls in love, but they're from different ☐ backgrounds. ☐ cities.	A scientist creates ☐ a new medicine. ☐ a scary monster.	A son helps his father find ☐ a criminal. ☐ a wife.

B Think of a movie. Write the type of movie, the setting, and one sentence about the story on a separate piece of paper.

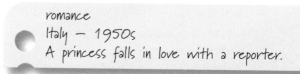

> romance
> Italy — 1950s
> A princess falls in love with a reporter.

C Work in groups. Take turns talking about your movies. Don't say the titles. Can your partners guess?

A It's a *romance*. The story takes place in *Italy in the 1950s*. It's about *a princess* who *falls in love with a reporter*.

B Is it *Roman Holiday*?

A Yes! You're right.
> **or**
> Sorry! Guess again.

💬 Talking about movies

Type of movie

It's a	romance. thriller. drama. documentary.	**It's a(n)**	action sci-fi horror	**movie.**

Setting

The story takes place in Italy in the 1950s.
It's set in New York City today.

Story

It's about a princess **who** falls in love.
Audrey Hepburn **plays** a princess **who** falls in love.

70 *Unit 6*

2 Movie reviews

A Read the list of words to describe movie features. Then add three more words.

Words to describe movie features

awful	moving	ridiculous	terrible	_____
✓ fantastic	powerful	shocking	terrifying	_____
hilarious	realistic	spectacular	thought-provoking	_____

B 🔘 38 Listen to the movie reviews. Did the reviewers like (☺) or dislike (☹) the features? Circle the correct answers.

Reviewer 1

acting	story	soundtrack
☺ ☹	☺ ☹	☺ ☹
fantastic	_____	_____

Reviewer 2

cinematography	special effects	acting
☺ ☹	☺ ☹	☺ ☹
_____	_____	_____

Reviewer 3

story	cinematography	dialog
☺ ☹	☺ ☹	☺ ☹
_____	_____	_____

C 🔘 38 Listen again. Write the word from the box in Exercise A that the reviewers use to describe each feature.

3 My movie review

Complete the chart with information about a movie you know. Then tell a partner about the movie.

Title	Features I liked	Features I didn't like
Batman Begins	acting — fantastic special effects — spectacular	soundtrack — terrible

*"I saw **Batman Begins**. The acting was fantastic, and the special effects were spectacular. But the soundtrack was terrible."*

Organization focus

1 Jason's movie review

A Look at the movie scenes. Do you know the movie? What do you think Jason will say about the movie?

B Read Jason's brainstorming notes for his movie review. Check (✓) the seven topics he included in his outline on page 73.

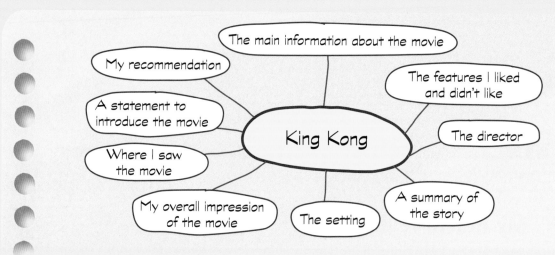

My recommendation

The main information about the movie

The features I liked and didn't like

A statement to introduce the movie

King Kong

The director

Where I saw the movie

A summary of the story

My overall impression of the movie

The setting

C Read Jason's additional notes for his movie review. Then use his notes to complete the outline on page 73.

- Naomi Watts and Jack Black
- action movie
- See it on a big screen.
- special effects were spectacular

- New York City
- incredibly powerful
- Denham captures King Kong, brings him to New York
- 1930s

2 Jason's outline

 39 Listen to Jason's movie review. Check the notes you added from Exercise 1C on page 72.

King Kong

I. Introduction

   A. A statement to introduce the movie: All movie audiences love a big, strong hero.

   B. The main information about the movie

      1. title: King Kong

      2. type of movie: _____

      3. lead actors: _____

II. Body

   A. The setting

      1. place: _____

      2. time: _____

   B. A summary of the story

      1. filmmaker Carl Denham goes to Skull Island to make a movie

      2. King Kong falls in love with lead actor, saves her from people and dinosaurs

      3. _____

      4. King Kong escapes, causes panic, finds Ann, climbs Empire State Building

   C. The features I liked and didn't like

      1. _____

      2. acting was excellent

      3. dialog was boring, movie was too long

III. Conclusion

   A. My overall impression of the movie

      1. absolutely fantastic

      2. _____

   B. My recommendation: _____

Presentation focus

1 Introduction

A Notice the information Jason included in the introduction of his movie review on page 75.

> ▶ A statement to introduce the movie
>
> *All movie audiences love . . .*
>
> ▶ The main information about the movie, such as the title, type of movie, lead actors

B 💿 40   Guess the missing words in Jason's introduction. Then listen and check your guesses.

2 Body

A Notice the information Jason included in the body of his movie review on page 75.

> ▶ The setting
>
> ▶ A summary of the story
>
> ▶ The features he liked and didn't like

B 💿 41   Guess the missing words in the body of Jason's movie review. Then listen and check your guesses.

3 Conclusion

A Notice the information Jason included in the conclusion of his movie review on page 75.

> ▶ His overall impression of the movie
>
> *Overall, I thought (movie) was . . .*
>
> ▶ His recommendation
>
> *My recommendation is . . .*

B 💿 42   Guess the missing words in Jason's conclusion. Then listen and check your guesses.

King Kong

Introduction

All movie audiences love a big, _____ hero — even if the hero is a giant gorilla! Maybe some of you can guess the title of the movie. It's _King Kong_. _____ an action movie, and it stars Naomi Watts and Jack Black.

Body

The story takes _____ in New York City in the 1930s. It's _____ a filmmaker named Carl Denham who goes to a place called Skull Island to make a movie. On the island, King Kong, a giant gorilla, falls in love with the lead movie actor, Ann Darrow. King Kong saves Ann from the people on the island and from some very scary dinosaurs. Denham wants to bring King Kong back to the United States and use him to make money, so he and his men capture King Kong and bring him back. But King Kong escapes, runs through New York looking for his sweetheart, Ann, and causes panic. When King Kong finally finds Ann, he climbs to the top of the Empire State Building. As you may know, the movie has an incredibly sad ending.

There were a lot of things I liked about _King Kong_. The special _____ were absolutely spectacular. The scenes in New York looked surprisingly realistic, and Skull Island was extremely scary. The _____ was excellent, too, especially the scenes with Naomi Watts and King Kong. Unfortunately, the _____ was a little boring in some parts, and the movie was too long.

Conclusion

Overall, I thought _King Kong_ was _____ fantastic. It was _____ powerful. My recommendation is: See it on a big screen — if you don't mind sitting for three hours.

Presentation skills focus

1   Using stress and emphasis with *absolutely*, *extremely*, *incredibly*, and *surprisingly*

When you describe the features of a movie, use intensifiers to make your description more interesting and exciting.

A 🔘 43   Listen. Notice the intensifiers. Then listen again and repeat the sentences.

1

2

3

4

The cinematography was *absolutely* fantastic.

The dialog was *extremely* thought-provoking.

The acting was *incredibly* moving.

The special effects were *surprisingly* realistic.

B 🔘 44   Listen to more people describe movies they have seen. Match the two parts of each sentence.

1. I thought the soundtrack was   _____ incredibly terrifying.

2. The story of *Frankenstein* was   _____ surprisingly awful.

3. The dialog was   _____ absolutely spectacular.

4. The music and dancing were   _____ extremely moving.

5. I thought the cinematography was   _1_ absolutely terrible.

> ### Presentation tip
> To make your description even more interesting, say the intensifiers more loudly than the rest of the sentence.

2 Your turn

A Think of a movie you know. Write the title below. Then write four sentences to describe its features. Use *absolutely, extremely, incredibly,* and *surprisingly.*

Note	• It is not common to use *absolutely* with the following words: *realistic, moving, powerful, thought-provoking.* • It is not common to use *extremely* with the following words: *awful, fantastic, spectacular, terrible.*

Movie title: _____

1. _____

2. _____

3. _____

4. _____

B Work with a partner. Take turns describing your movies from Exercise A.

"I saw X-Men. I thought the costumes were incredibly realistic."

C Read the example from a movie review. Underline the intensifiers.

The best movie I've ever seen is *Titanic*. What a great movie! The costumes and the scenery were incredibly beautiful, and the special effects were surprisingly realistic. I felt like I was on the ship myself! I thought the soundtrack was absolutely fantastic, too. My favorite thing about the movie was the story, though. The love story between the two main characters, Jack and Rose, was incredibly romantic. I thought Leonardo DiCaprio's acting was extremely powerful, especially at the end when he saves the life of his true love.

D Take turns reading the example in Exercise C aloud. Practice using intensifiers with stress and emphasis.

Now **present yourself!**

- **Turn to page 78.**
- **Prepare your presentation.**

Present yourself!

1   Brainstorming

Choose a movie you've seen. Write the title in the center of the brainstorming map. Then add as many details as you can for each brainstorming topic.

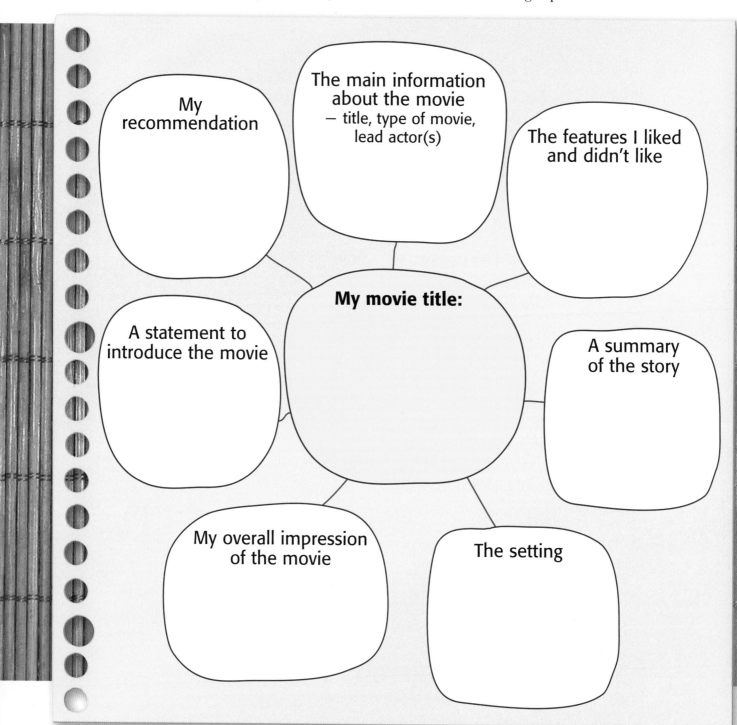

My recommendation

The main information about the movie — title, type of movie, lead actor(s)

The features I liked and didn't like

My movie title:

A statement to introduce the movie

A summary of the story

My overall impression of the movie

The setting

2 Organizing

Use your brainstorming notes from Exercise 1 to complete the outline. Then make note cards from your outline and practice your presentation.

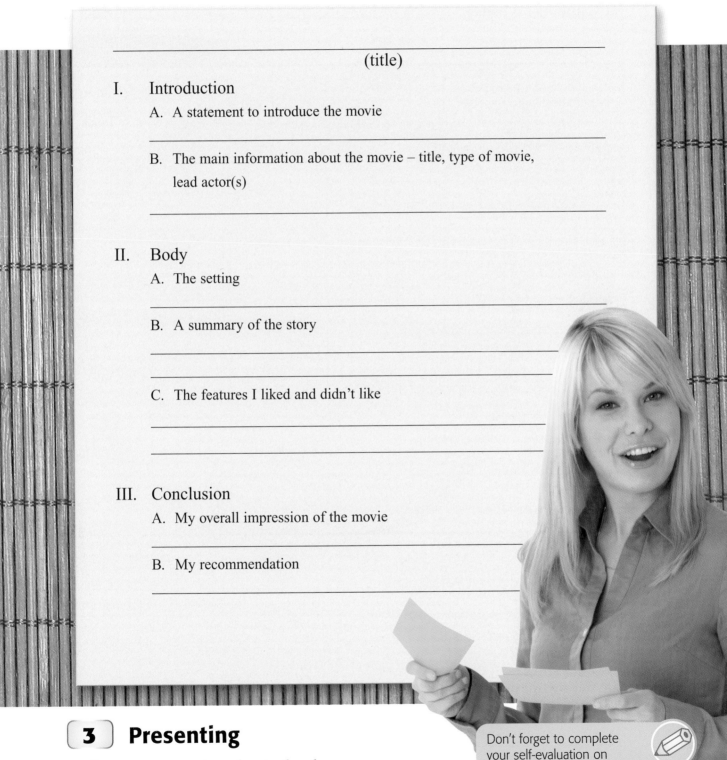

_____
(title)

I.   Introduction

A. A statement to introduce the movie

_____

B. The main information about the movie – title, type of movie, lead actor(s)

_____

II. Body

A. The setting

_____

B. A summary of the story

_____

_____

C. The features I liked and didn't like

_____

_____

III. Conclusion

A. My overall impression of the movie

_____

B. My recommendation

_____

3 Presenting

Present your movie review to the class. Remember to use the intensifiers *absolutely*, *extremely*, *incredibly*, and *surprisingly*.

Don't forget to complete your self-evaluation on page 85 after your presentation.

Unit 1 Self-evaluation

A classmate introduction

Read each statement. Circle, ☺, ☻, or ☹. Then write comments that will help you improve next time.

		Comments
I included information about my classmate that was interesting to my audience.	☺ ☻ ☹	
I practiced enough before giving my presentation.	☺ ☻ ☹	
I included all the points from my notes in my presentation.	☺ ☻ ☹	
I used the stage presence techniques from the *Presentation skills focus* lesson on page 16.	☺ ☻ ☹	
My presentation was the right length.	☺ ☻ ☹	
I felt confident when giving my presentation.	☺ ☻ ☹	
I said "thank you" at the end of my presentation.	☺ ☻ ☹	
I am satisfied with my presentation.	☺ ☻ ☹	

One thing that I did well was _____

_____

_____ .

One thing that I would like to do better for my next presentation is _____

_____

_____ .

A favorite place

Read each statement. Circle ☺, ☺, or ☹. Then write comments that will help you improve next time.

		Comments
I chose a place that was interesting to my audience.	☺ ☺ ☹	
I practiced enough before giving my presentation.	☺ ☺ ☹	
I included details about my favorite place that were interesting to my audience.	☺ ☺ ☹	
I used gestures for describing size and shape from the *Presentation skills focus* lesson on page 28.	☺ ☺ ☹	
I looked at the audience during my presentation.	☺ ☺ ☹	
My presentation was the right length.	☺ ☺ ☹	
I felt confident when giving my presentation.	☺ ☺ ☹	
I am satisfied with my presentation.	☺ ☺ ☹	

One thing that I did well was _____

_____

_____ .

One thing that I would like to do better for my next presentation is _____

_____

_____ .

A prized possession

Read each statement. Circle, ☺, ☺, or ☹. Then write comments that will help you improve next time.

		Comments
I chose a possession that was interesting to my audience.	☺ ☺ ☹	
I practiced enough before giving my presentation.	☺ ☺ ☹	
I showed my possession to the audience so they could see it clearly.	☺ ☺ ☹	
I gave a good explanation of why my possession is important to me.	☺ ☺ ☹	
I used the show-and-tell expressions from the *Presentation skills focus* lesson on page 41.	☺ ☺ ☹	
My presentation was the right length.	☺ ☺ ☹	
I felt confident when giving my presentation.	☺ ☺ ☹	
I am satisfied with my presentation.	☺ ☺ ☹	

One thing that I did well was _____

_____

_____ .

One thing that I would like to do better for my next presentation is _____

_____

_____ .

A memorable experience

Read each statement. Circle, ☺, ☺, or ☹. Then write comments that will help you improve next time.

		Comments
I chose an experience that was interesting to my audience.	☺ ☺ ☹	
I practiced enough before giving my presentation.	☺ ☺ ☹	
I introduced my experience in an interesting way.	☺ ☺ ☹	
I gave a good explanation of how I felt during the experience.	☺ ☺ ☹	
I used the intensifiers *really*, *so*, and *very* from the *Presentation skills focus* lesson on page 52.	☺ ☺ ☹	
My presentation was the right length.	☺ ☺ ☹	
I felt confident when giving my presentation.	☺ ☺ ☹	
I am satisfied with my presentation.	☺ ☺ ☹	

One thing that I did well was _____

_____

_____ .

One thing that I would like to do better for my next presentation is _____

_____

_____ .

Unit 5 Self-evaluation

Show me how.

Read each statement. Circle, ☺, ☺, or ☹. Then write comments that will help you improve next time.

		Comments
I chose a topic that was interesting or useful to my audience.	☺ ☺ ☹	
I practiced enough before giving my presentation.	☺ ☺ ☹	
I introduced each step clearly with *First . . . , Next . . .* , etc.	☺ ☺ ☹	
I looked at my audience often to check that they could follow the steps.	☺ ☺ ☹	
I used expressions for emphasizing key points from the *Presentation skills focus* lesson on page 65.	☺ ☺ ☹	
My presentation was the right length.	☺ ☺ ☹	
I felt confident when giving my presentation.	☺ ☺ ☹	
I am satisfied with my presentation.	☺ ☺ ☹	

One thing that I did well was _____

_____

_____ .

One thing that I would like to do better for my next presentation is _____

_____

_____ .

Movie magic

Read each statement. Circle, ☺, ☺, or ☹. Then write comments that will help you improve next time.

		Comments
I chose a movie that was easy for me to talk about.	☺ ☺ ☹	
I watched the movie more than once and made notes.	☺ ☺ ☹	
I practiced enough before giving my presentation.	☺ ☺ ☹	
I told the audience about the features I liked and didn't like.	☺ ☺ ☹	
I used the intensifiers *absolutely*, *extremely*, *incredibly*, and *surprisingly* from the *Presentation skills focus* lesson on page 76.	☺ ☺ ☹	
My presentation was the right length.	☺ ☺ ☹	
I felt confident when giving my presentation.	☺ ☺ ☹	
I am satisfied with my presentation.	☺ ☺ ☹	

One thing that I did well was _____

_____

_____ .

One thing that I would like to continue to work on in the future is _____

_____

_____ .

Acknowledgments

Illustration Credits

Phil Hankinson: 12, 22, 46
P. Hoey: 34, 58, 59
Jui Ishida: cover
Rui Ricardo: 3, 6, 16, 28, 40, 52, 64, 76

Photographic Credits

2 ©Inmagine.
5 ©Inmagine.
8 *(clockwise from top left)* ©Inmagine; ©Ghislain & Marie David de Lossy/Getty Images; ©Inmagine; ©Inmagine.
10 *(left to right)* ©Inmagine; ©Dimitri Vervitsiotis/Getty Images; ©Inmagine.
11 *(left to right)* ©Shutterstock; ©Inmagine.
13 *(top to bottom)* ©Getty Images; ©Shutterstock.
15 ©Shutterstock.
19 ©Dennis Kitchen Studio Inc.
20 *(left to right)* ©Inmagine; ©Burazin/Getty Images; ©Jon Mikel Duralde/Alamy.
21 *(top to bottom)* ©istockphoto; ©istockphoto.
23 ©Inmagine.
24 *(left to right)* ©David Young-Wolff/Photoedit; ©Shubroto Chattopadhyay/Photolibrary.
25 ©Harvey Schwartz/Photolibrary.
27 ©Shutterstock.
31 ©Dennis Kitchen Studio Inc.
32 *(clockwise from top left)* ©Shutterstock; ©Rodolfo Arpia/Alamy; ©Inmagine; ©Inmagine; ©Inmagine; ©Dorling Kindersley/Getty Images; ©istockphoto; ©Inmagine.
33 ©Shutterstock.
35 ©Inmagine.
36 ©Inmagine.
37 ©bluemagenta/Alamy.
39 ©Shutterstock.
43 ©Dennis Kitchen Studio Inc.
44 *(clockwise from top left)* ©Henryk Kaiser/Photolibrary; ©Inmagine; ©Inmagine; ©Inmagine.
45 *(top to bottom)* ©Inmagine; ©Shutterstock.
48 ©dbimages/Alamy.
49 *(top to bottom)* ©David R. Frazier Photolibrary Inc./Alamy; ©Inmagine.
51 ©Shutterstock.
55 ©Dennis Kitchen Studio Inc.
56 *(clockwise from top left)* ©UpperCut Images/Getty Images; ©Inmagine; ©istockphoto; ©Inmagine; ©Inmagine; ©Dorling Kindersley/Getty Images; ©Shutterstock; ©Dorling Kindersley/Getty Images.
57 ©Inmagine.
61 ©Image100/Photolibrary.
63 ©Inmagine.
67 ©Dennis Kitchen Studio Inc.
70 *(left to right)* ©Everitt Collection; ©Mirisch-7 Arts/United Artists/Kobal; ©TriStar/Everitt Collection.
72 ©Universal/Everitt Collection; ©Universal/Everitt Collection.
73 ©Evan Agostini/Getty Images.
75 ©Inmagine.
79 ©Dennis Kitchen Studio Inc.

Audio CD track listing

The audio CD contains the audio exercises for *Present Yourself 1, Experiences.*

Unit	Page	Exercise	Track
Getting ready	3	2B	2
Getting ready	5	2B	3
1	10	1A	4
1	11	3B	5
1	13	2	6
1	14	1B	7
1	14	2B	8
1	14	3B	9
2	22	1A, 1B	10
2	23	2B	11
2	25	2	12
2	26	1B	13
2	26	2B	14
2	26	3B	15
3	34	1A	16
3	35	2A	17
3	37	2	18
3	38	1B	19
3	38	2B	20
3	38	3B	21

Unit	Page	Exercise	Track
4	46	1A, 1B	22
4	47	2A, 2B	23
4	49	2	24
4	50	1B	25
4	50	2B	26
4	50	3B	27
4	52	1A	28
4	52	1B	29
5	58	1A	30
5	58	1B	31
5	59	2A	32
5	61	2	33
5	62	1B	34
5	62	2B	35
5	62	3B	36
6	70	1A	37
6	71	2B, 2C	38
6	73	2	39
6	74	1B	40
6	74	2B	41
6	74	3B	42
6	76	1A	43
6	76	1B	44